Foreword

In an age when the conduct of all professionals is under constant scrutiny, it is vital for Scottish solicitors to act in accordance with best professional practice. Over the years, professional practice has been regulated by professional practice rules, guidance notes issued by the Law Society of Scotland and by the decisions of the discipline tribunal in regard to what it perceives as professional misconduct. However there has long been a need for a comprehensive and authoritative guide to professional conduct.

Jane Ryder is well qualified to provide this. A solicitor who has practised in Scotland for fifteen years and has been an active member of the Council of the Law Society of Scotland for eight years, she readily responded to the invitation of the Council to prepare this work which is based on her detailed experience of the work of the Council and its committees.

I am particularly pleased to see that the author has not only provided examples from the fields of conveyancing and litigation, but has also introduced commercial and corporate examples of issues such as confidentiality and conflict of interest, which are so topical. I am also pleased to see the emphasis on practice management, which is reflected in the Council's own guidance manual *Better Client Care and Practice Management* issued to the profession in 1995. Taken together, these publications at last provide a comprehensive and up-to-date guide to best professional practice and I have no doubt that both will be of enormous value to the profession.

Alan Boyd
Edinburgh

June 1995

Professional Conduct for Scottish Solicitors

Jane Ryder MA
Solicitor

Butterworths/Law Society of Scotland
Edinburgh
1995

United Kingdom	Butterworths, a Division of Reed Elsevier (UK) Ltd, 4 Hill Street, EDINBURGH EH2 3JZ and Halsbury House, 35 Chancery Lane, LONDON WC2A 1EL
Australia	Butterworths Pty Ltd, SYDNEY, MELBOURNE, BRISBANE, ADELAIDE, PERTH, CANBERRA and HOBART
Canada	Butterworth Canada Ltd, TORONTO and VANCOUVER
Ireland	Butterworth (Ireland) Ltd, DUBLIN
Malaysia	Malayan Law Journal Sdn Bhd, KUALA LUMPUR
New Zealand	Butterworths of New Zealand Ltd, WELLINGTON and AUCKLAND
Puerto Rico	Butterworths of Puerto Rico Inc, SAN JUAN
Singapore	Malayan Law Journal Pte Ltd, SINGAPORE
South Africa	Butterworth Publishers (Pty) Ltd, DURBAN
USA	Butterworth Legal Publishers, CARLSBAD, California, and SALEM, New Hampshire

Law Society of Scotland
26 Drumsheugh Gardens, EDINBURGH EH3 7YR

A CIP Catalogue record for this book is available from the British Library.

ISBN 0 406 04498 8

Typeset by Phoenix Photosetting, Chatham, Kent.
Printed and bound in Great Britain by Mackays of Chatham PLC, Chatham, Kent

Acknowledgments

This book has been eight years in the making in the sense that it reflects my experience as a Council member of the Law Society. My thanks are therefore due to all Council members – past and present – without whom this work would never have been written. My thanks are also due to the numerous individual solicitors who have provided comments and advice, and who have stimulated debate and discussion, informing, supporting and participating in the collective work of the Council and its committees.

The work of all members of the Secretariat is essential to the efficient operation of the Council and the profession, but I should extend particular thanks to Michael Clancy, David Cullen, Lindsay Paterson, Bruce Ritchie and Philip Yelland who read and corrected individual sections of the text. Thanks are also due to Les Bell for his expertise in insurance, to Gerry Brown and Paul Burns for comments on criminal matters, and to Gordon Davidson and Andrew Chalmers for stimulating debates on conflict of interest and on practice management. The expertise of Douglas Mill proved invaluable in discussing practice management and Alastair Thornton was particularly helpful on the role of the solicitor as officer of the court. They may not agree with all my conclusions: they certainly should not be held responsible for any errors, whether of fact or judgment.

Above all, Kenneth Pritchard as Secretary of the Law Society has advised, encouraged, warned and more besides. Anyone who has put into effect all his advice over the years probably has no need of this book, but I dedicate it to those like myself who doubt whether they have yet implemented his counsel of perfection.

Jane Ryder
Edinburgh

31 March 1995

Contents

Table of statutes

Table of orders, rules and regulations

Table of cases

Abbreviations

AC	Law Reports, Appeal Cases (House of Lords and Privy Council) 1890–
All ER	All England Law Reports 1936–
Ch	Law Reports, Chancery Division 1980–
ECR	European Court of Justice Reports 1954–
EHRR	European Human Rights Reports 1979–
GWD	Green's Weekly Digest 1986–
JLSS	Journal of the Law Society of Scotland
M	Macpherson's Session Cases 1862–73
Macq	Macqueen's House of Lords Reports 1851–65
NLJ	New Law Journal 1965–
R	Rettie's Session Cases 1873–98
SC	Session Cases 1907–
SC (HL)	House of Lords Cases in Session Cases 1907–
SCLR	Scottish Civil Law Reports 1987–
SLT	Scots Law Times 1893–
SLT (Notes)	Notes of Recent Decisions in Scots Law Times 1946–81
SLT (Sh Ct)	Sheriff Court Reports in Scots Law Times 1893–
Times	Times Law Reports
WLR	Weekly Law Reports 1953–

1. Introduction

The demographic and institutional profile of the solicitors' profession in Scotland has undergone significant change over the last 20 years. The traditional image of the solicitor may still be that of the elderly male partner in his book-lined office, but over 40 per cent of the profession are now under 40 and over 50 per cent of those recently admitted have been women. Most solicitors are still in private practice, and until five years ago one would have said that the trend was towards the creation of ever larger firms. However with the recession and a marked reduction in the number of assistants and indeed partners required by the established firms, there has been an upturn in the number of sole practitioners. In addition, there are increasing numbers of solicitors in the public service and commercial sector[1].

Issues of professional ethics and practice concern every solicitor, whether a partner in a practice with 100 or more staff, an assistant, a sole practitioner or an in-house company solicitor. While basic principles are common to all solicitors, some detailed regulations have only limited relevance for those in the public sector. Nevertheless it is the policy of the Council of the Law Society of Scotland to maintain a unitary profession, despite occasional divergence of views, for example over the relevance of the corporate advertising campaign of the early 1990s, and it is encouraging to see that in 1995 the President of the Law Society is a solicitor from the public sector.

The Code of Conduct for solicitors, issued by the Law Society, narrates in the preamble the Society's view that lawyers have a special role in a society founded on respect for the rule of law. As the preamble suggests, lawyers have moral as well as legal obligations, and these may sometimes appear to conflict. There is no disagreement that these obligations

---

1. For further details see Law Society of Scotland's consultation document 'A Review of the Training of Solicitors' December 1994.

co-exist, but there may be disagreement about the balance to be struck and it is the aim of this book to attempt to complement the Code, the Society's regulations and the Discipline Tribunal's decisions to enable the solicitor to decide how that balance can be achieved.

The dilemma exists at an institutional as well as an individual level, since the Law Society itself is charged with what may appear to be a statutory conflict of interest. In terms of the Solicitors (Scotland) Act 1980, s 1, the object of the Society includes the promotion of the interests of the solicitors' profession in Scotland and the interests of the public in relation to that profession. In most cases these interests coincide and the Society has been able to advance both the interests of the profession and the public, for example in criticism of cuts in legal aid and the introduction of new court fees. In addition the Society's detailed regulation of its members is in the public interest, particularly in maintenance of the Guarantee Fund and operation of the new compensation provisions for inadequate professional service. Nevertheless members of the public sometimes feel the Society is too anxious to protect the interests of its members: on the other hand solicitors frequently complain that the Society is not doing enough for its members. The Council continues to steer a difficult course between Scylla and Charibdis and it is hoped this book helps individual solicitors to do the same.

2. Requirements of practice

Regulation

The profession in Scotland is notionally self-regulating, but subject to increasing external regulation. The principal legislation is contained in the Solicitors (Scotland) Act 1980 and the Law Reform (Miscellaneous Provisions) (Scotland) Act 1990. In addition, there is a considerable body of subordinate legislation in the form of Practice Rules and Regulations made by the Council of the Law Society of Scotland.

The Council is authorised to make regulations for practical training, legal education and the passing of examinations in terms of the 1980 Act, s 5 with the concurrence of the Lord President. Under the 1980 Act, s 34 the Council may make rules to regulate the professional conduct, practice and discipline of solicitors, but only after consultation with the profession and with the approval of the Lord President. Breach of practice rules and regulations may amount to professional misconduct and may expose a solicitor to disciplinary action.

The Council does not however have an unlimited discretion. In particular, regulations may require separate approval by the Secretary of State[1] - and are of course open to challenge in the ordinary way, for example if in breach of natural justice[2]. Moreover solicitors undertake activities which are subject to indirect regulation by external bodies – solicitors conducting investment business, for example, are authorised by the Law Society as a self-regulating organisation. The Society is in turn recognised by the Securities and Investment Board (SIB) and the Society's Investment Business Practice Rules must meet with the adequacy standard required by the SIB. In addition

1. For example Solicitors (Scotland) (Multi-Disciplinary Practices) Practice Rules 1991.
2. *Pharmaceutical Society v Dickson* [1968] 2 All ER 686; see also *R v Chance ex p Smith* (1995) Times, 28 January.

solicitors are subject to general legislation such as the Property Misdescriptions Act 1991, the Data Protection Act 1984 and the Money Laundering Regulations 1993.

Admission as a solicitor

No person may practise as a solicitor unless they are admitted as a solicitor, have their name on the roll and hold a practising certificate issued by the Council[1]. The rationale was cogently stated by the Tribunal:

'The established procedure whereby a solicitor is required to obtain a practising certificate before he can practise or hold himself out to be solicitor is of long standing and the provisions are clearly set out in the Solicitors (Scotland) Act 1980. These provisions are for the protection of both other members of the profession and the public. The issuing of a practising certificate enables the Law Society to maintain a complete record which is open to public inspection containing the names of all solicitors who are so entitled to practise. . . .[2]'

To be admitted a candidate must satisfy the Council that he or she is over 21, has complied with the Society's regulations under s 5 and has obtained a certificate from the Council to the effect that they are a fit and proper person to be a solicitor. In terms of the Admission as a Solicitor (Scotland) Regulations 1986 a candidate must normally undertake either a degree in law at a Scottish university or enter into a three-year pre-Diploma training contract. In addition, a candidate must undertake a one-year Diploma course at a Scottish university and thereafter serve under a post-Diploma training contract. A training contract may not be entered into with a near relative[3] and there is a limit to the number of trainees a firm may employ at any one time[4]. There are special provisions for other EC-qualified lawyers to be admitted as solicitors in Scotland[5]. The training of solicitors was the subject of a wide-ranging consultation document issued by the Law Society in December

1. Solicitors (Scotland) Act 1980, s 4.
2. Re F J Feely 1993 JLSS 242.
3. Admission as a Solicitor (Scotland) Regulations 1986, reg 14 (2).
4. Admission as a Solicitor (Scotland) Regulations 1986, reg 14 (4).
5. EC Qualified Lawyers Transfer (Scotland) Regulations 1990.

1994 and it is likely that changes will be introduced, particularly as regards the content of the Diploma course and the adequacy and supervision of the training received by trainees.

In theory the Society exercises authority only over its members. It has no power as such to regulate the activities of persons who are no longer on the roll of solicitors, although it is an offence for a person who has been struck off the roll or suspended from practice as a solicitor to accept employment with a solicitor's practice without informing the employer[1]. A solicitor who, without the consent of the Council, knowingly employs or remunerates a person who has been struck off or is suspended from practice as a solicitor is liable to be struck off or suspended[2]. It is also important to note that claims on the Guarantee Fund may be made notwithstanding the fact that – as is often in fact the case – the solicitor has been struck off the roll or has ceased to practise or been suspended from practice[3]. It is also possible to make a finding of inadequate professional service (IPS) against a solicitor even where he or she has been struck off the roll of solicitors, ceased to practise or been suspended from practice[4].

It is an offence for any person to practise or hold themselves out as a solicitor without having in force a practising certificate, unless it can be proved that the person acted without receiving or without any expectation of any fee, gain or reward, directly or indirectly[5]. This is to be distinguished from the proposition that a solicitor is always required to render an adequate professional service, whether or not the solicitor renders a fee and irrespective of the level of fee charged[6]. In addition, failure on the part of a solicitor in practice to have in force a practising certificate may be treated as professional misconduct[7] and may attract disciplinary proceedings leading to suspension[8]. In certain circumstances an applicant must give the Council notice of not less than six weeks of the intention to

1. Solicitors (Scotland) Act 1980, s 28.
2. Ibid, s 47.
3. See p 7.
4. 1980 Act, s 42A(8); see pp 146–147.
5. 1980 Act, s 23(1).
6. For adequate professional services see pp 40–44.
7. 1980 Act, s 23(2).
8. Re FJ Feely 1993 JLSS 242.

apply for a practising certificate, and the Council may grant or refuse the application or issue a certificate subject to such conditions as it thinks fit[1].

It is an offence for an unqualified person to draw or prepare writs relating to heritable or moveable estate, to any action or proceedings in court or any papers on which to found or oppose an application for a grant of confirmation in favour of executors ('the reserved areas'[2]) although there are certain limited exceptions[3]. It is also an offence for a solicitor to act in such a way as to enable an unqualified person to appear, act or practise in any respect as a solicitor or notary public[4]. The statutory prohibition against a solicitor sharing fees derived from any solicitor's business transacted by him or her with unqualified persons[5] was repealed with effect from March 1993 but there is still a prohibition in the Practice Rules, and there are rules against multi-disciplinary partnerships[6]. The cumulative effect of these provisions is that, in addition to the Society regulating the conduct of members, there is also an element of indirect regulation of the activities of persons other than members.

Practice as a solicitor

Any solicitor whose name is entered on the roll is required to advise the Council of his or her place of business and of any change of address. Solicitors must also comply with the disclosure requirements of the Companies Act 1981, s 29, both as regards all business stationery and the display of notices within business premises. Solicitors registered for VAT must disclose their VAT registration number and generally comply with all their statutory duties as employers, for example under the Health and Safety Acts. Physical injuries in the workplace, including repetitive strain injury to typing staff, are obviously

1. 1980 Act, s 15.
2. Ibid, s 32(1).
3. Ibid, s 32(2)-(3).
4. Ibid, s 26.
5. Ibid, s 27.
6. Solicitors (Scotland)(Multi-Discipline Practices) Practice Rules 1991.

the concern of all employers but other issues such as stress-related illnesses should be of increasing concern to employers of professionals.

Solicitors must comply with detailed rules regulating the keeping of accounts, conduct of investment business etc which are considered elsewhere[1]. Two of the most important practical requirements for the operation of solicitors' practices arise from the 1980 Act, ss 43 and 44. Under s 43 the Society is required to maintain a Guarantee Fund to be held for the purpose of compensating persons who, in the opinion of the Council, suffer pecuniary loss by reason of dishonesty on the part of a solicitor (notwithstanding the fact that the solicitor may have been struck off the roll or may have ceased or been suspended from practice as a solicitor). All principals in private practice are required to contribute to the Fund, which has been subject to a number of large claims in recent years. Claims may be made upon the Guarantee Fund where insurance is not available and where the cause of loss is dishonesty. The usual situation giving rise to claims is where there is dishonesty by a sole practitioner (where, by definition, there are no partners and therefore no insurance cover available). However claims may also be made on the Guarantee Fund where the insurance cover, together with the personal assets of all the partners, is not sufficient to meet relevant claims[2].

Under the 1980 Act, s 44 the Council has the power to make rules concerning professional indemnity insurance for solicitors. At the time of writing the Society has in place a Master Policy with selected insurers (in contrast to the situation in England where the Law Society of England and Wales maintains a mutual insurance fund). The minimum level of cover which a practice (including a sole practitioner) must maintain is £1,000,000 although many practices take out 'top-up cover' over and above this amount. Whatever the financial difficulties for the practice, the solicitor has a duty to ensure there are specific funds to finance the practice, including the premium for professional indemnity insurance, and the only acceptable alternative to having insurance is to withdraw from practise[3].

---

1. See chapters 11–13.
2. Scottish Solicitors Guarantee Fund Rules 1985.
3. Re GC Gillespie 1994 JLSS 224.

Cover under the Master Policy is on a claims made basis, and for their own protection it is therefore prudent for outgoing partners to insist upon remaining partners maintaining the same level of cover for the prescriptive period after retiral.

Practitioners

Solicitors may choose to practise in a number of different ways:

(1) **As sole practitioners.** With the recession of the 1990s the number of sole practitioners has substantially increased. The category of sole practitioners includes so called 'freelance' solicitors who may be working part time and whose clients tend to be other solicitors' firms rather than members of the public. Nevertheless where they are self-employed, they are sole practitioners and as such are required to contribute to the Guarantee Fund and to maintain professional indemnity insurance.

(2) **As partners in private practice.** Traditionally the position to which most solicitors have aspired, although for the foreseeable future the supply of law graduates far exceeds demand for their services in private practice[1]. Certainly it is no longer uncommon for partners to move to different firms (giving rise to problems with mandates and transfer of business[2]). Any person wishing to set up in private practice must, unless he or she has been a principal within the five years preceding the date of setting up in practice or already attended such a course, attend a practice management course within twelve months of becoming a principal[3]. In England a solicitor of less than three years' standing may not practise from an office as a principal[4]; at the time of writing there is no such restriction in Scotland, but when this was discussed at the 1995 AGM there was overwhelming support for the introduction of restrictions.

1. Law Society's consultation document 'A Review of the Training of Solicitors' December 1994.
2. See pp 49–50.
3. Solicitors (Scotland) (Attendance at Courses on Practice Management) Practice Rules 1989.
4. Solicitors Practice Rules 1975.

(3) **As an incorporated practice.** Although partnership is the traditional vehicle for solicitors in private practice, it is possible for solicitors to incorporate[1]. At the time of writing there have only been two incorporated practices set up in Scotland, but other professions, for example accountants, are seriously considering the option of incorporation and it may be that more solicitors' firms will follow their example. The various disciplinary, insurance and Guarantee Fund rules apply to incorporated practices as well as to partnerships, while the memorandum and articles of the company must be approved by the Society and may not be altered without the prior written consent of the Council. The approved memorandum and articles will contain an article restricting membership to holders of practising certificates or recognised incorporated practices[2], and restrictions on the transfer of shares[3].

(4) **As consultants.** Traditionally, although not necessarily, the retired senior partner of a practice, which wishes to preserve its particular client base for the practice. The consultant is not in partnership with a solicitor, but is considered a part of the practice unit for the purposes of insurance, and is not therefore required to maintain separate cover. The consultant must hold a practising certificate[4] and his or her status must be unambiguously stated on professional stationery so as to be distinguished clearly from the partners[5].

(5) **As an associate**. Provided the individual holds a practising certificate free of conditions imposed by the 1980 Act or the Discipline Tribunal, the Council has no locus to intervene and the designation of associate is conferred by the employing solicitor. The 1989 Rules refer to the 'status' of associate and it is normally given to a senior assistant. As such, it may be a factor in deciding what degree of supervision should be exercised and what confidence a member of the public should place in the associate. It has been suggested that employers who are

1. Solicitors (Scotland)(Incorporated Practices) Practice Rules 1987.
2. Ibid, Sch 2, Form A, art 14. See also Form B, art 4 and Form C, art 14.
3. Ibid, Form A, art 15. See also Form C, art 15.
4. Solicitors (Scotland) (Associates etc) Practice Rules 1989, r 2; Solicitors (Scotland) Act 1980, s 21.
5. Solicitors (Scotland) (Associates etc) Practice Rules 1989, r 5.

obliged to settle negligence claims arising out of the actings of associates and employees generally might recover their uninsured loss from these employees: the author's view is that the problem is usually one of supervision and lack of systems, and recovery from an employee would be unprofessional conduct on the part of employers, although internal disciplinary proceedings (and ultimately termination of employment) may be appropriate. The position would be different where the claim arose out of fraud or dishonesty.

(6) **As employees in private practice.** Although the assistant solicitor is supervised by a partner, the Tribunal has made it clear that assistants cannot 'blindly follow the directions of the principal solicitor' and disregard the ethical consequences of any of their actings. Assistants must balance their duties to their employer with their own professional responsibilities[1]. This may present severe practical difficulties for employees, even at the risk of their employment. If faced with such a dilemma, employees should feel free to consult the Law Society or any Council member for help and guidance.

(7) **Within the commercial or public sector, as a salaried employee.** There are a growing number of solicitors in this category, which may include procurators fiscal, sheriffs, solicitors for local authorities, banks and building societies as well as in-house commercial lawyers. Since they do not handle clients' funds they are not liable to contribute to the Guarantee Fund, nor do the Accounts Rules apply. However they are subject to the same rules as regards professional misconduct[2]. The Law Society of England and Wales takes the view that a solicitor who takes strike or other industrial action in breach of a contract of employment is prima facie guilty of unbefitting conduct, but whether this justifies disciplinary proceedings depends on the circumstances[3]. In Scotland, a solicitor is entitled to take industrial action, but subject to an overriding duty to fulfil any professional duties to the courts or Parliament, and any personal obligations undertaken other than those

---

1. Tribunal decision 809/90.
2. But see pp 59–60.
3. *The Professional Conduct of Solicitors* para 3-02

imposed under the terms and conditions of employment. The solicitor is also required to take all reasonable steps to secure the consent of those organising industrial action to his or her continuing to act, where a failure to act could result in danger to the public or serious damage to a party other than his or her employer[1]. There has been only one prosecution of a public sector solicitor before the Discipline Tribunal in Scotland: presumably on the basis that most employers large enough to employ solicitors directly have their own disciplinary procedures and rely on these rather than pursue a complaint through the Law Society.

Practice management

The solicitor who is a partner in private practice quite clearly has a personal interest in ensuring that the business is efficient, in the sense that it is well organised in order to maximise profit. This interest extends to all employees, whether in the private or public sector, since employees of any enterprise run the risk of redundancy if they are not performing their duties efficiently and, as a result, the business is not making sufficient profit. As noted elsewhere[2] the Law Society is entitled to apply for appointment of a judicial factor to any firm which is insolvent or where the books and accounts are in such condition that it is not reasonably practicable to ascertain definitely whether or not the firm is solvent[3].

However the desirability of efficient practice management is also firmly grounded in the solicitor's duty to render an adequate professional service to the client and indeed to honour professional obligations to the client and third parties, including the profession itself. The distinction may be drawn between adequate practice, including practice management, which is required of all solicitors, and best practice which is desirable but not essential. It is not a solicitor's professional duty to maintain a practice as efficiently as it is possible to do

1. Solicitors (Scotland) Practice Rules 1981
2. See p 118.
3. Solicitors (Scotland) Act 1980, s 41.

so: provided the solicitor provides an adequate service to clients and observes other professional duties, the Law Society cannot insist that the solicitor demonstrates that the practice (provided technically solvent) is profitable or, for instance, uses ultra-modern technology. However examples of how inefficient practice management can impact upon performance of those professional duties appear throughout this book.

There is no definitive model. It should also be stressed that, although formal quality assurance systems such as BS5750/ISN 9000 have considerable merit (and may come to be required, for example in the context of compulsory competitive tendering) they are not a guarantee of the quality of legal advice. What efficient operational systems and practice management can achieve is to minimise the risk of administrative errors, as opposed to errors of judgment, bearing in mind that most professional negligence claims against solicitors arise from missed time bars and errors of detail rather than errors of law.

Whether the solicitor's firm elects for independent accreditation, or chooses its own model, the primary duty is to run a practice which is efficient enough to enable the solicitor to perform his or her professional duties as outlined in this book, and to fulfil any contractual obligations undertaken in terms of the solicitor's partnership or contract of employment. With this in mind, it is a requirement that any solicitor who becomes a principal in a practice unit must, within twelve months of becoming a principal, attend a practice management course[1]. The solicitor is exempt from this requirement if he or she has been a principal at any time within the preceding five years: as the Rules came into effect in 1989 any solicitor now becoming a principal is caught by the requirement to attend a course, whether or not they benefit from the exemption on joining a practice unit as a principal. It is also an ongoing requirement for all solicitors, whether partners or not, to comply with the Solicitors (Scotland) (Continuing Professional Development) Regulations 1993. Initially restricted to those qualified for less than ten years, by November 1996 these Regulations will apply to all solicitors holding a practising certificate. Continuing

---

1. Solicitors (Scotland)(Attendance at Courses on Practice Management) Practice Rules 1989.

professional development for this purpose means not simply an awareness of developments in the law but also management and organisation, communication and client care skills and other relevant areas designed to improve an individual's ability to operate properly and effectively as a solicitor. Quite specifically, no less than five hours of the total annual requirement (of which a minimum of three hours must be group study) must be spent on training in management (including self-management) organisation, client care and communication skills. As the Regulations and guidelines make clear, business skills such as financial and business management, budget control, setting priorities and time management are all part of the practice management skills which a solicitor requires in addition to technical legal competence.

Particularly useful in this context are the Law Society of Scotland's guidance manual *Better Client Care and Practice Management*[1], a guide written by practising solicitors, and the Law Society of England and Wales' draft code of quality management, developed with a view to BS5750 accreditation.

Staff supervision and partners' actings

Supervision of staff is perhaps no more than a critical aspect of practice management. Clearly the solicitor cannot provide an adequate service to clients without an efficient staff, which includes not only assistants and trainees but paralegals and secretarial and administrative staff. Obligations of confidentiality, disclosure and reporting apply to the whole practice unit and not merely the partners, and there should be an adequate system to ensure that the staff are aware of these issues and can, for example, identify a conflict of interest or a potential money laundering and know how to act in such a situation. Many firms maintain an office manual with written procedures (of little value unless kept up to date) and there are numerous guidance manuals available[3]. The recognition of the particular importance of staff to a solicitor's practice has led a

---

1. Law Society of Scotland, May 1995.
2. Including the Law Society's *Better Client Care and Practice Management*.

number of firms to join formal training quality initiatives such as Investors in People, either in conjunction with, or even in preference to, procedural quality assurance systems such as BS5750/ISN 9000.

A partner/officer may delegate to a junior member of staff but must exercise the appropriate level of supervision to ensure that the standard of work is not less than would be expected of a legally qualified and competent solicitor, since a claim for professional negligence lies against the firm rather than the individual. The dangers of inadequate supervision are reflected in professional indemnity insurance premiums: because of the incidence of claims against firms with high part-ner:staff ratios, a loading is imposed on the insurance premi-ums of those firms where partner:staff ratios exceed the average. Failure to adequately supervise may also result in a finding of professional misconduct: the failure to provide ade-quate supervision can itself amount to professional miscon-duct on the part of the principal, but it is also no defence to a charge of professional misconduct that the principal was unaware of the improper actings of an employee. The Tribunal has held that a solicitor who delegates work has a duty of supervision and must accept personal responsibility for improper actions which result from a failure to supervise[1].

Every partner is an agent for the firm and has implied authority in terms of the Partnership Act 1890 to bind the firm. As a matter of law anyone other than a partner does not have implied authority, and a third party is entitled to be satisfied that the person signing on behalf of a firm has authority[2]. However it is established practice that only a partner should validly subscribe the firm name on a document purporting to be holograph of the firm[3].

Principals should also be aware that they have responsibili-ties to staff as well as to clients in ensuring proper allocation of work and adequate training, supervision and support of staff. If the Council decides after due inquiry that a solicitor is not fulfilling the proper obligations of an employer under a train-ing contract either in relation to a particular contract or

1. *MacColl v Council of the Law Society of Scotland* 1987 SLT 525.
2. Cusine and Pearson ' Who signs on behalf of the firm' 1991 JLSS 73.
3. *Littlejohn v Mackay* 1974 SLT (Sh Ct) 82.

generally, it may notify the solicitor's firm that it may not thereafter engage or retain the services of any trainee without the
special consent in writing of the Council[1]. The Society also has
the power after inquiry to grant a certificate of fitness at its own
hand where the employer has acted unreasonably in refusing
to grant a certificate[2] and to call upon the solicitor to discharge
or assign the contract where the trainee and employer are in
dispute[3].

Where there is a prima facie case of professional misconduct,
for example where there has been a breach of the Accounts
Rules, there may be no professional misconduct on the part of
any partners who have not been an active party to such a breach.
Where there has been dishonesty on the part of one of the partners or employees it can be particularly difficult to determine
the culpability of the other partners, who may have benefited to
the extent of enhanced fees but without being aware that there
was any impropriety. However it is not enough for the partners
merely to have turned a blind eye; for example although each
firm must appoint a designated cash room partner in terms of
the Solicitors (Scotland) Accounts Rules 1995, the Rules make it
clear that each partner of the firm is responsible for securing
compliance with the Accounts Rules, and a partner has to show
more than mere inattention to escape a charge of professional
misconduct[4]. In *Sharp v Council of the Law Society*[4] the Inner
House held that it was essential in every case to consider the
whole circumstances and the degree of culpability attached to
the individual complained of.

Multi-discipline partnerships

A distaste for the concept of the multi-discipline practice is
shared by most of the professions in the UK, including both the
Scottish and English Law Societies, on the basis that all professions wish to preserve not only their financial independence,
but their different codes of conduct and professional ethics.

1. Admission as a Solicitor (Scotland) Regulations 1986, reg 14(3).
2. Ibid, reg 33.
3. Ibid, reg 35(2).
4. *Sharp v Council of the Law Society of Scotland* 1984 SLT 313.

The degree of protection for their clients which solicitors in Scotland can demonstrate, through the Guarantee Fund and professional indemnity insurance arrangements, was seen as significant in the 1989 debate as to whether reserved areas should be opened up to non-qualified persons. At that time there was also a perceived threat that solicitors' firms would be absorbed by the larger accountants', and it was recognised that there were possibly insuperable difficulties in reconciling different professional standards and practices, not least with professional indemnity insurance.

While there are significant differences between the professional codes of solicitors and accountants, particularly with regard to conflict of interest and confidentiality, solicitors who are involved in larger commercial transactions face problems of practice and ethics which are more familiar to those accountants dealing with similar transactions than to solicitors dealing with say matrimonial problems or criminal matters. It seems desirable that, so far as consistent with the professional ethics of each profession, there should be a common approach over matters such as confidentiality and contingency fees and the professions in Scotland are establishing a series of joint working parties to look at this.

The former statutory prohibition against solicitors sharing fees with non-qualified persons[1] was repealed by the Law Reform (Miscellaneous Provisions) (Scotland) Act 1990 although the prohibition still exists by virtue of the Solicitors (Scotland) Practice Rules 1991. Moreover the creation of multidiscipline practices is also prohibited by the Solicitors (Scotland) (Multi-Disciplinary Practices) Practice Rules 1991. In terms of rule 3 a solicitor is not permitted ' to form a legal relationship with a person or body who is not a solicitor with a view to their jointly offering professional services as a multidisciplinary practice to any person or body'. Accordingly a solicitor may not enter into a partnership with other professionals, for example accountants. The Incorporated Practice Rules require that memorandum and articles of the company restrict membership to persons holding a practising certificate.

Nevertheless a solicitor cannot of course be prevented from employing surveyors, accountants or other professionals and

---

1. Solicitors (Scotland) Act 1980, s 27.

awarding bonuses to employees from time to time, so achieving a multi-discipline practice in all but name. There is an argument that this is even more attractive from the employees' point of view, since they are not thereby exposed to the possibility of unlimited liability which partnership attracts although it should be remembered that, if business is conducted through the medium of a company, any professional, whether solicitor or not, might fall to be treated as a shadow director for the purposes of the Companies Acts.

3. International practice

Practice outwith Scotland

Since European law is a part of Scottish domestic law, and since so much legislation, for example company and revenue law, is intra-UK it is increasingly difficult to define the work of the Scottish solicitor as advising on purely Scottish law. A solicitor who wishes to practise as a principal within Scotland must provide the Law Society with evidence of professional indemnity insurance before his or her annual practising certificate is issued. The Master Policy provides professional indemnity insurance for any legal work 'normally carried out by a Scottish solicitor' and this wording is sufficiently flexible to cover not only any transactions with a European dimension and cross-border transactions with England which necessarily require a knowledge of 'UK' law, but also expansion into new areas, such as sponsorship of USM companies[1] or commercial lobbying, provided these fall within the class of work normally undertaken.

There is no requirement under the Master Policy that the work be undertaken within Scotland, if the solicitor is offering advice on Scottish law as broadly defined. Scottish solicitors can offer advice on Scottish law from a Scottish base or from the offices of the Law Society in Brussels. Subject to Master Policy restrictions and provided the host jurisdiction allows, firms are also free to set up their own offices outside Scotland and several have done so. The Law Society of England and Wales currently rules that firms who have dual qualified partners may not use the Scottish firm name when trading in the English reserved areas, unless there is a direct connection between the names of the firm and the names of the partners. The Law Society of Scotland imposes no such restriction on a firm practising in Scotland.

1. (1994) *Independent* 29 November.

The Master Policy provides a Scottish principal with cover in respect of advice given on foreign law provided the advice is given by a person qualified to give that advice, for example a French or German qualified solicitor. However the Master policy does not provide cover for residence or physical representation in the USA or Canada (irrespective of the fact that the solicitor is advising on Scottish law) while brokers' advice should be taken on any work within Scotland which originates in any US or Canadian jurisdiction. The Master Policy obviously covers solicitors for proceedings in Scotland, including enforcement of foreign judgments, but not for that element of a Scottish transaction which involves any punitive or exemplary damages originating in a US or Canadian jurisdiction.

Establishment in the European Union

Under the Treaty of European Union, lawyers are self-employed persons who have a right to provide legal services on a temporary or occasional basis in another member state, or to establish themselves or their firm in another member state on the same basis as nationals of that country. However barriers to free movement may be imposed where this is justifiable on certain enumerated grounds, and it is fair to say that the current position is thoroughly confused as to where and in what circumstances foreign lawyers are entitled to establish themselves in the various member states.

The UK has the most liberal policy and there are no restrictions on a foreign national offering legal services within the UK, subject to the fact that only appropriately qualified UK solicitors can practise in the 'reserved areas'. At the time of writing, almost all the foreign firms in Scotland are English firms, but in London in particular there are numerous foreign firms, some operating as branches and some as principal offices.

A Scottish solicitor wishing to establish an office within the jurisdiction of another member state might encounter more difficulties. After protracted negotiation, the Council of the Bars and Law Societies of the European Community (CCBE) had thought the text of a draft Establishment Directive agreed, but the formal draft Establishment Directive published in December 1994 departed significantly from the CCBE draft. In particular it provides that any lawyer might establish an office under the title of his or her home bar within the jurisdiction of another state (the host state) but that after a five-year residence, the lawyer is no longer permitted to carry on as a temporary resident and is required to be admitted as a member of the relevant professional body within that host state - a sort of compulsory naturalisation process. This applies even where the lawyer only practised the law of his or her home state or international law. The Directive envisages that the lawyer gains access to the legal profession of the host member state either by showing an unbroken period of at least three years activity involving the law of the host member state, or by passing an exam in the procedural law and deontology of the host member state (or by sitting an aptitude test under the Mutual Diplomas Directive). From the point of view of the consumer, the drawback appears to be that the lawyer may thereby become entitled to the designation of lawyer in the host member state without necessarily having to meet the aptitude criteria which would apply if the lawyer sought to qualify by the formal route of seeking to have his or her qualifications recognised under the Mutual Recognition Directive.

Whether the limitation on the right to establishment under home title is restricted or not, there is no doubt that there are difficulties and inconsistencies with regard to rules of professional conduct and professional indemnity insurance which requires detailed consideration and possible amendment of domestic legislation and internal regulations and procedures of all European law societies. Meanwhile, the European Court has already ruled that the promulgation of professional rules, such as a prohibition on advertising, is a matter for internal regulation by each member state[1] although the liberal professions are not considered exempt from competition rules[2].

Provision of services and cross-border practice

There are likely to be fewer difficulties where the Scottish lawyer merely wishes to advise on an occasional basis,

1. *Casado Coca v Spain* [1994] 18 EHRR 1; see p 101.
2. C/046/M/B/COAPI; see p 101.

although in some jurisdictions the lawyer may have to be designated, for host jurisdiction purposes, as a legal adviser or consultant rather than solicitor. If the services rendered are not within the 'reserved areas' of a member state, a European host country cannot insist on a local lawyer appearing alongside the visiting lawyer[1] although the visiting lawyer must respect the rules of the host country as well as those of his or her own Bar (the double deontology rule). A Scottish solicitor conducting cross-border practice is required to observe and be bound by the Code of Conduct[2] which is reproduced as a Schedule to the Solicitors (Scotland) (Cross-Border Code of Conduct) Practice Rules 1989. 'Cross-border' means all professional contacts with lawyers of member states of the European Community other than the United Kingdom and the professional activities of a solicitor in a member state of the European Community, other than the United Kingdom, whether or not the solicitor is physically present in that member state. The purpose of the Code is to mitigate the difficulties which arise from the application of 'double deontology', although there may still be occasions where the rules of one Law Society or Bar conflict with those of the host member state.

The Code itself takes precedence over domestic regulations, since rule 1.3.2 expressly states that:

'After the rules in this code have been adopted as enforceable rules in relation to his cross border activities the lawyer will remain bound to observe the rules of the Bar or Law Society to which he belongs *to the extent that they are consistent with the rules in this code.* '[3]

It is less easy to establish whether home or host rules should take precedence where these (as opposed to the lawyers themselves) are in conflict. Firstly it should be noted that the Rules impose a duty on lawyers 'to inform themselves as to the rules which will affect them in the performance of any particular activity'[4] which may include the extent to which a lawyer may

---

1. Case 427/85 EC *Commission v Federal Republic of Germany* [1988] ECR 1123.
2. Ie the Code of Conduct for lawyers in the European Community adopted by the Bars and Law Societies of the European Community on 28 October 1988, to be distinguished from the CCBE Code of Conduct adopted by the Law Society and reproduced as Schedule 1 to the Code of Conduct (Scotland) Rules 1992.
3. Author's italics.
4. Code, r 2.4.

engage in incompatible occupations, advertising etc. The position with regard to fees and clients' funds is relatively clear cut: fees are to be charged specifically in accordance with the rules applied to members of the Bar or Law Society to which the lawyer belongs, and if he or she belongs to more than one Bar or Law Society the rules applied are those with the closest connection to the contract between the lawyer and client[1]. Funds are to be held in accordance with the rules of the host member state, unless with the agreement of the competent authorities of both home and host member state, the lawyer elects to comply with the requirements of the host member state (in which case the lawyer is required to specifically inform clients of the election)[2].

Otherwise the explanatory memorandum provides that a lawyer acting in the restricted areas shall 'observe the rules of professional conduct of the host Member State, without prejudice to his obligations in the Member State from which he comes'[3] while a lawyer pursuing activities which are not within the restricted areas, 'remains subject to the conditions and rules of professional conduct of the Member State from which he comes, without prejudice to respect for the rules, whatever their source, which govern the profession in the host Member State. . .'. The memorandum goes on to state (one can hardly say to clarify) that:

'The latter rules are applicable only if they are capable of being observed by a lawyer who is not established in the host Member State and to the extent to which their observance is objectively justified to ensure, in that state , the proper exercise of a lawyer's activities, the standing of the profession and respect for the rules concerning incompatibility.'

'Capable of being observed' must mean something more than 'are not a breach of professional rules of the Member State from which the lawyer comes' or there would be no need to elaborate on the extent to which observance may be justified. It is not certain who would be the arbiter of 'objectively justified': it is suggested this is one occasion on which the Tribunal would require to hear evidence as to proper professional conduct[4].

1. Code, r 3.4.2.
2. Code, r 3.8.3.
3. General Principles, r 2.4.2.
4. See p 29.

Exclusions

The Cross-Border Practice Rules do not apply to the work of notaries. In most other European countries notaries are public officials who authenticate deeds etc and who are not actively involved in the sort of litigation and negotiation which are the subjects of the Code. It appears that under the provisions of the EC Treaty, article 55, notaries as public officers are also exempt from the Establishment Directive[1].

Note also that the Public Notaries Act 1801 restricts notarial activity in England to those admitted as notaries in England. It is suggested that although this means English-based Scottish notaries should not undertake notarial acts in England in respect of documents which are intended to be produced in the English courts, a Scottish notary should not be precluded from undertaking notarial acts in respect of documents which are to be produced in Scottish proceedings or transactions. If the notary attesting the execution is not in fact a Scottish notary, the Scottish court may be entitled to request an 'apostille' or authentication of the notary's signature by the Foreign and Commonwealth Office. It is fair to say the point has rarely if ever been taken, but this may be an area that would benefit from a little judicious law reform. It should be remembered that whereas English courts frequently require the production of sworn affidavits, the Scottish courts tend to rely on ex parte applications.

The Cross-Border Practice Rules specifically exclude intra-UK transactions, although in fact when most Scottish lawyers refer to cross border transactions they tend to mean transactions which involve Scotland and England. The formal position with regard to English/Scottish cross-border transactions is distinctly unsatisfactory although common perceptions and convergence of authority mean there are relatively few practical problems in the conduct of transactions.

Multi-national partnerships

In contrast to the multi-disciplinary partnership, most European law societies have accepted the principle of the

1. Committee on Notaries Public 5.10.1994.

multi-national partnership and the draft Establishment Directive specifically requires each member state (with limited exceptions) to make provision for at least one legal form in which lawyers, including lawyers from different member states, can practise jointly. In Scotland, the Law Reform (Miscellaneous Provisions)(Scotland) Act 1990, s 60A already permits solicitors and incorporated practices to enter into multi-national practices with registered foreign lawyers, subject to the Council maintaining a register of such lawyers and making rules as to registration. The rules require to be approved by the profession and the Lord President in the usual way, while the Secretary of State may by order made by statutory instrument provide that any enactment relating to solicitors shall apply to registered foreign lawyers.

Little forward progress has been made with the elaborate formal framework envisaged by s 60A. Meanwhile, the Solicitors (Scotland) Practice Rules 1991 has extended the definition of lawyer, with whom a solicitor may share fees, to include

'a member of the Faculty of Advocates in Scotland or a legal practitioner offering services to the legal public who is qualified and licensed to practice in accordance with the law of a legal jurisdiction other than Scotland, and includes a firm of lawyers, a law centre, a European Economic Interest Group the membership of which is exclusively lawyers, an incorporated practice of lawyers and any association (whether corporate or unincorporate) consisting exclusively of lawyers or exclusively of lawyers and solicitors.'[1]

The uncertainty with regard to the Financial Services Act and the difficulties thrown up by the Cross-Border Practice Rules and the Establishment Directive suggest that it may be some considerable time before there are any formal international standards for multi-national partnerships established. As noted earlier rules of the Law Society of England and Wales currently prohibit multinational firms of Scottish solicitors with English partners from practising under certain names in England (although not vice versa). Meanwhile, many solicitors' firms now belong to international legal groups which give access to international contacts and through which they

---

1. Solicitors (Scotland) Practice Rules 1991, r 2(1).

are developing international business links and are able to share fees on the basis of the 1991 Practice Rules. It may well be that these groups will develop uniform administrative structures and economies of scale, to deliver many of the advantages of the multi-national partnership in all but name and none of the disadvantages of joint and several liability and conflict of interest.

4. Rules of professional conduct

Moral standards?

The nature of the rules of professional conduct or professional ethics is the subject of considerable debate. Are these rules moral standards or merely a regulatory framework? There is no doubt that there have been significant changes even in the last ten years. When the last professional guide was published in conjunction with the Law Society, there was no Code of Conduct, no Conflict of Interest Rules and no compensation for inadequate professional service. The view of the authors was that 'Rules for professional conduct are designed to ensure that high professional standards are maintained for the good both of the profession and the public'[1].

Interestingly the Code of Conduct now places the emphasis on performance and regulation:

'Rules of professional conduct are designed to ensure the proper performance by a lawyer of a function which is recognised as essential in all civilised societies. The failure of a lawyer to observe these rules must in the last resort result in a disciplinary action.'

In face of the proliferation of written rules and the increasing emphasis on the service element of legal services, it can now be argued that professional ethics has become a matter of practice and procedure, and the rules of professional conduct are now disciplinary tools rather than moral aspiration.

There is certainly an increasing emphasis on proper performance in the sense of competence. Further consideration is given to the provision of professional services in chapter 5[2] but given the requirement to attend practice management courses and to undertake continuing professional education, and above all the Society's power to order compensation for inade-

1. Webster *Professional Ethics and Practice for Scottish Solicitors* (1984) para 1-03.
2. Pages 40–44; see also pp 146–147.

quate professional services, it may be that the technical standards required are higher than ever before.

Written or unwritten?

Until relatively recently the Council of the Law Society set itself against too many written rules, on the basis that it was better to set out general principles and to give the Society (and ultimately the Discipline Tribunal) flexibility in determining what constituted professional misconduct. Indeed there is no doubt that the profession continues to be regulated by unwritten rules of conduct as well as written rules. In one of the most important recent decisions, Lord President Emslie defined professional misconduct as, in effect, a consensus:

'There are certain standards of conduct to be expected of competent and reputable solicitors. A departure from those standards which would be regarded by competent and reputable solicitors as serious and reprehensible may properly be categorised as professional misconduct. Whether or not the conduct complained of is a breach of the rules or some other actings or omissions the same question falls to be asked and answered. . . .'

That consensus is now embodied in a written Code of Conduct and numerous specific rules. The Code of Conduct is the general Code of Conduct of the CCBE (Council of the Bars and Law Societies of the European Community) agreed in 1989 and adopted by all the Bars and law societies of the member states and observer members. The Code is intended to be taken into account in all revisals of national rules with a view to progressive harmonisation of professional practice rules for lawyers[2]. The International Bar Association's updated International Code is also a useful statement of basic principles and, significantly, the IBA has now agreed that it will not introduce any new clauses which might be at odds with the CCBE Code.

For Scotland alone, there are separate rules for solicitor-advocates[3] and a separate Code of Conduct for solicitor-mediators. Finally there are the numerous specific rules to which

1. *Sharp v Council of the Law Society of Scotland* 1984 SLT 313.
2. 1989 SLT (News) 261.
3. See pp 86–88.

reference is made throughout. Many of these rules, for example Accounts Rules are no more than detailed expressions of common law principles of agency, but all are aimed at the maintenance of high professional standards.

Questions of conduct

Serious breaches of either statutory rules or of the commonly perceived rules of good practice and behaviour amount to professional misconduct, a concept which the courts have been reluctant to define but ready to recognise:

'I shall not attempt to define professional misconduct. But if the statutory tribunal composed as it always is of professional men of the highest repute and competence stigmatise a course of professional conduct as misconduct, it seems to me that only strong grounds would justify this court in condoning as innocent that which the Committee have condemned as guilty.'[1]

It is immaterial whether the professional misconduct follows from a breach of the practice rules or not: the test is whether the conduct complained of is sufficiently serious to amount to misconduct in the sense that it represents a deaparture from the standards of conduct 'to be expected of competent and reputable solicitors'. As the passage quoted earlier makes clear, it is a departure from the standards which would be regarded by competent and reputable solicitors as serious and reprehensible which may properly be categorised as professional misconduct and ' in every case it is essential to consider the whole circumstances and the degree of culpability which ought properly to be attached to the individual against whom the complaint is made'[2].

Although it is the Society which refers complaints to the Discipline Tribunal, it is the Discipline Tribunal (formerly known as the Discipline Committee) which ultimately rules on matters of professional misconduct. The Tribunal considers that its members, who include a majority of solicitors together with a minority of lay members, themselves have the

1. Lord President Cooper in *E v T* 1949 SLT 411.
2. *Sharp v Council of the Law Society* 1984 SLT 313.

necessary expertise to decide on what is misconduct without hearing evidence on this point from witnesses including a former President of the Law Society[1].

In assessing whether a course of action amounts to professional misconduct, the Tribunal takes into account the degree of culpability of the solicitor in all the circumstances. It may not be necessary for active participation to be proved to establish professional misconduct[2]. In *Council of the Law Society v J*[3] it was held that 'the circumstances' could never include the fact that the solicitor was ignorant of a new practice rule which had only recently come into force. Where breaches of the rules were by an employee who had acted without a solicitor's knowledge, this could still amount to professional misconduct[4].

In appropriate cases the Society or the Tribunal may take the view that conduct is not sufficiently serious to be professional misconduct and instead may make a finding of unprofessional conduct. The conduct complained of will be conduct which, while not amounting to professional misconduct, cannot be approved and will include incidents where solicitors fail to meet accepted standards of courtesy or behaviour in the course of their professional dealings, for example being rude to clients or fellow professionals.

However solicitors may also be disciplined for professional misconduct (and exceptionally for unprofessional misconduct) for aspects of their private life. It has been held that 'a solicitor is required to maintain the same standard of propriety in his private life and in relation to any commercial ventures as are expected of him in his professional practice'[5], and to act 'in a manner consistent with membership of an honourable profession'[6]. As contemporary attitudes change, so will the perception of what is or is not acceptable in a solicitor; for example although minor motoring offences are technically criminal offences, they are generally disregarded. On the other hand,

1. Tribunal decision 761/89.
2. Tribunal decision 723/87.
3. 1991 SLT 662.
4. *MacColl v Council of the Law Society of Scotland* 1987 SLT 525.
5. Tribunal decision 768/89.
6. *United Bank of Kuwait v Hammoud* [1988] 3 All ER 418 at 430 per Lord Donaldson, referred to in Tribunal decision 768/89.

while a sexual relationship with a client is unlikely to be a criminal offence, it is inadvisable, not least because it lays the solicitor open to charges of undue influence and a lack of independence. Such a relationship is likely to be considered professional misconduct: however the Society and the Tribunal would certainly find it hard to achieve any consensus with regard to sexual relationships outside the solicitor-client relationship. While adultery might have been considered dishonourable at one time, most younger members of the profession would hardly consider adultery in itself (as opposed to domestic violence or abuse) a disciplinary matter nowadays. On the other hand, younger members in particular would no longer find any degree of sexual comment, harassment or intimidation, in or out of the office, acceptable or amusing.

In Scotland it is not professional misconduct as such for a solicitor to have outside business interests, although this may be a contractual issue if deemed to distract the solicitor from any obligations in a partnership agreement or contract of employment. It may also impinge on the independence of solicitors and the impartiality of their advice. European jurisdictions differ on the extent to which a lawyer may engage in other occupations and in conducting cross-border business solicitors should have regard to the provisions of the Cross-Border Code of Conduct[1].

Where someone (correctly) designates themself as a solicitor, it is competent for the Society or Tribunal to exercise their powers even where the solicitor is not practising as such: for example where a solicitor, the sole director of an English company which was compulsorily wound up, was severely criticised by the Court of Appeal, including a criticism that he had mislead investors[2]. It seems likely that disciplinary proceedings would be maintained against, say, a solicitor-director disqualified under the Company Directors Disqualification Act 1986.

Personal financial difficulties are more problematic: it may well be that a solicitor finds him or herself in financial difficulties which lead to legal proceedings and, ultimately, may lead

1. Solicitors (Scotland) (Cross-Border Code of Conduct) Practice Rules 1989, Sch, r 2.5.
2. Tribunal Decision 768/89.

to sequestration. If the estate of a solicitor is sequestrated, or a solicitor grants a trust deed for behoof of creditors or a judicial factor is appointed on the estate of the solicitor under the 1980 Act, s 41, the solicitor's practising certificate automatically ceases to have effect and the solicitor is suspended from practice[1]. The suspension is lifted on the discharge, but in the meantime the solicitor may also apply to the Council to terminate the suspension. The Council considers the circumstances of the financial collapse and if the solicitor is not deemed culpable, the certificate may be renewed. On one view, any financial collapse to some extent brings the profession into disrepute and may call into question the financial judgment of the solicitor. On the other hand, the solicitor in private practice is not immune to economic pressures common to all small to medium-size businesses and it is hardly surprising that in a market place where there is too great a supply, too little demand and considerable pressure on profit margins some solicitors' firms should suffer. If the solicitor is sequestrated but the certificate is renewed on application, it will almost certainly be on condition that the solicitor is restricted to practising as an assistant and not as a principal, so there is a sanction even where the solicitor is permitted to recommence practice.

New applicants for admission are required to disclose any convictions, however minor, and the Society interviews those with convictions before deciding whether or not they will be admitted in terms of the Admission Regulations. In general, minor convictions, for example for breach of the peace while a student, do not prevent admission, but the Council is reluctant to admit any applicant with any conviction for dishonesty or financial mismanagement.

1. Solicitors (Scotland) Act 1980, s 18.

5. Relationship with the client

Taking instructions

A solicitor is normally free to decide whether or not to accept instructions from a particular client although refusal to act must not be on the basis of race, colour or ethnic origins. The English Code of Conduct states that a solicitor should not accept instructions where the solicitor suspects that those instructions have been given by a client under duress or undue influence, making it clear that the solicitor must be satisfied that the instructions were freely given by seeing the client alone, or the solicitor must refuse to act. This would be a relevant consideration where, for example, a spouse or relative was granting a standard security for another's business debts.

However, a solicitor is not free to act where there is a conflict of interest or breach of confidentiality and where the solicitor has a personal interest in the transaction, for example where a testator wishes to leave a bequest to the solicitor. The solicitor may therefore be required to withdraw from acting before conclusion of a transaction in certain circumstances. Conflict of interest is considered in greater detail in chapter 8.

Relationship with the client

Solicitors should know their clients. In some circumstances it may be critical to know the client's matrimonial status – when purchasing domestic property, for example, the solicitor must know whether or not to obtain a consent under the Matrimonial Homes Act 1983. A solicitor in commercial transactions may be asked to provide an opinion letter which may include confirming that documents are signed in accordance with the company memorandum and articles and that the company has the power to borrow. In each case the solicitor should be satisfied as to the status and authority of the party giving instructions.

Where advising more than one party, for example husband and wife or partners, the solicitor should be aware of the possibility of a conflict of interest[1] and where appropriate should remind parties of their right to independent advice. It would almost certainly be negligent for a solicitor not to advise a spouse to seek independent advice before granting a standard security over the matrimonial home as security for the business debts of the other spouse, although banks may not have a similar obligation at law[2]. Where instructions are received via an intermediary, for example from a bank or estate agent, the position should be checked with the client as soon as possible[3]. Where acting for separated spouses when a jointly owned dwellinghouse is to be sold, a solicitor selling the property should be quite clear to have binding instructions from both the parties as to the division of the proceeds of sale. The selling solicitor may not accept instructions from one of the parties to arrest funds due to the other party and a client who insisted on issuing such an instruction must be referred to a different firm. It is not permissible to refer the client to a different solicitor within the same firm. Where agreement has not been reached as to the division of proceeds of sale, there is clearly potential for conflict of interest and the Law Society Guidelines require a different firm, independent of those instructed in the matrimonial dispute, to be instructed in the sale[4].

The solicitor has a specific duty to know the client in order to comply with the Investment Business Rules and the Money Laundering Regulations, which are considered elsewhere. Many firms maintain a database for their own purposes, but should be aware of the provisions of the Data Protection Act 1984 as well as the common law duty of client confidentiality (although there are specific exceptions to client confidentiality under the Money Laundering Regulations and earlier legislation, as discussed in chapter 13).

Solicitors should clearly establish the extent of their instructions. Where a solicitor-mediator undertakes the conduct of

1. See chapter 8.
2. *Mumford v Bank of Scotland; Smith v Bank of Scotland* 1994 SLT 1288.
3. Practice Note 1983 JLSS.
4. Law Society Guidelines 1994.

alternative dispute resolution there is a written appointment and in other cases a fee-charging agreement may also operate as a letter of authority. It may also be useful to prepare a written case plan, or at the very least a written check list: it is certainly good practice to record the client's specific instructions not only as an aide memoire at the time but also to be used in the unfortunate event of any later disagreement. It has been held that the facts must be ascertained before determining whether the client is bound by an offer in settlement on the basis that the solicitor has ostensible authority to settle a litigation proceeding in the Court of Session[1]. Where a solicitor concludes a contract without authority, the solicitor may be liable not only to the client but to an aggrieved third party in contract as well as delict, where there is an implied warranty given by the solicitor that the principal has given instructions[2].

The solicitor should deal with the client's business without undue delay and should keep the client informed of progress. By far the largest number of complaints received by the Law Society relate to solicitors' delay, to their failure to respond to letters and telephone calls, and generally to their failure to advise clients what is happening. Failure to act promptly can amount to serious misconduct and has the potential to cause serious prejudice to the client, for example failure to record a disposition or a security, or failure to register a charge with the Registrar of Companies. Not only is failure to correspond a want of courtesy, it may now in itself amount to IPS (and in extreme cases to unprofessional conduct or misconduct).

Without patronising the client, the solicitor should nevertheless take care to ensure that communications are comprehensible. What is appropriate language for one client may not be appropriate for another. At the opposite extreme, the solicitor should also take care that he or she does not become too familiar with the client, although clients may of course develop into personal friends. The parties should remain aware that the relationship is one of solicitor and client: the fact that they are on first name terms or even that the services are being rendered free of charge does not mean that there may not be IPS, unprofessional conduct or misconduct.

1. *Wight Civil Engineering Ltd v Parker* 1993 GWD 974.
2. Gloag *Contract* p 155; *Merrick Homes v Duff* 1994 GWD 1731.

Where a solicitor acts as agent for another solicitor in conducting a litigation, there is a duty owed to the client as well as the instructing solicitor, although correspondence should normally be conducted through the solicitor principal. If undertaking work for a new correspondent it is prudent for the solicitors to make clear at the outset what each expects of the other and to establish who has primary conduct of the action. For an ongoing transaction, the solicitor acting as agent should not accept direct instructions from the client without the knowledge and consent of the instructing solicitor, but the consent of the original solicitor is no longer required where a client wishes to instruct the agent directly in relation to a subsequent transaction[1].

A solicitor should always explore with the client the possibility that legal aid and/or legal advice and assistance may be available to both parties and the consequences, particularly if the action is to be defended[2]. The solicitor should also make it clear to the client that any sums recovered may be subject to repayment to the Compensation Recovery Unit and should be aware of the effect that the CRU claw back provisions may have on sums which may be received by the client. However unpalatable, it is a fact, as has been pointed out[3] that there comes a point where the accumulation of benefits has a material effect on the conduct of litigation, irrespective of the merits of any claim[3].

In any litigation, it should be made clear to the client at what stage he or she is expected to pay court fees and other outlays, and the consequences if the client finds him or herself unable to fund an action which has already started. This is particularly important given recent changes to the structure and level of court fees. It should also be made clear to the client that there may be a shortfall between recoverable judicial expenses and the solicitor-client account. The solicitor may also want to explore the possibility of a conditional fee-charging agreement and a written fee-charging agreement[4].

---

1. Professional Practice Committee 4.4.1991.
2. *Ness Gallagher v Sharples* 2 September 1994, unreported.
3. F Maguire 'Compensation recovery' 1994 JLSS 455.
4. See p 110.

Termination of the relationship

The client may always terminate the solicitor-client relationship at any time. In contrast, the solicitor should not cease to act for clients unilaterally and without good cause. However there are circumstances in which it is legitimate to withdraw from acting, for example if the client does not wish to accept the solicitor's advice or in any other circumstances where there has been a breakdown in the basis of trust which is necessary for the solicitor-client relationship. In some circumstances, for example where there is a conflict of interest, the solicitor has no choice but to withdraw from acting. Where a solicitor does withdraw from acting, this should be done at such a time and in such a way as not to prejudice the interests of the client. A solicitor should not normally withdraw from a complicated case the day before a proof or hearing when it would be impossible for another solicitor to come to grips with the case and take over within the designated timetable, although there may be exceptional circumstances when this is unavoidable[1]. A solicitor should normally have done sufficient preparation in advance of a complicated case so as not to be in this position at such a late stage. If it should have been obvious at a much earlier stage that there was, for instance, an inherent conflict of interest, the solicitor may rightly be criticised for only considering this and/or taking action to withdraw at a late stage.

Where a solicitor has declined to accept instructions at the outset, or has withdrawn from acting, this should be made quite clear to the client, particularly if there are time limits which are due to expire (for example a claim for personal injuries) or court hearings are scheduled[2]. For this reason, there is a professional duty upon the solicitor to advise a client in writing that the file will be closed in the absence of instructions within a specific period of time[3]. Termination of the solicitor-client relationship may cause particular problems where a legal aid certificate is to be transferred: for mandates and ownership of papers see chapter 6.

---

1. For example if a solicitor-advocate were called upon to conduct a criminal trial.
2. See A Newbold 'A solicitor's liability to "potential" clients' Law Society's Gazette 2.12.1987.
3. Professional Practice Committee 2.7.1992.

Independence

Rule 1 of the Code of Conduct is unequivocal:

'Independence is essential to the function of solicitors in their relationships with all parties and it is the duty of solicitors that they do not allow
their independence to be impaired irrespective of whether or not the matter in which they are acting involves litigation.'

The Code interprets independence to mean that solicitors must
not allow themselves to be restricted in their actings on behalf
of or in giving advice to their clients, nor must they allow
themselves to be influenced by motives inconsistent with the
principles of the Code. The solicitor should be aware of the
possibility that independence may be compromised not only
by external intervention but more insidiously; for example a
solicitor who is dependent upon a single client may find it difficult to give the client unpalatable advice. This caveat must be
balanced against the benefits of establishing a good working
relationship with a client. The Accountants Code recognises
the over-dependence on a single client by ruling that a firm
may not derive more than 15 per cent of gross practice income
from audit or recurring work for a single client, or 10 per cent
where the client is a listed or other public interest company.
These are 'the extremes beyond which the public perception of
a member's objectivity is likely to be at risk' and practices are
recommended to consider the propriety of accepting further
instructions once fees from a particular client exceed 10 per
cent of gross practice (or 5 per cent for a listed company or
other public interest company)[1]. Although there is no similar
detailed provision in the Law Society rules, it is a useful guideline and it is certainly worth a solicitor considering what the
effect on the practice would be if the single largest client with-
drew instructions.

Other areas of risk include significant overdue fees, loans to
or from clients and acceptance of hospitality. A firm's objectivity may be threatened when it is involved or even threatened
with litigation in relation to a client and the availability of

---

1. ICAS *Guide to Professional Ethics* 1992 p 8.

disciplinary proceedings can be open to abuse. It is worth noting that the Company Law Committee tends to the view that a speculative fee-charging agreement is not appropriate for a solicitor acting in a company acquisition or contested takeover, on the basis that the solicitor might be tempted to accept otherwise doubtful conditions in order to see the transaction proceed, whereas the accountants take the view that a speculative basis is acceptable since the client might not otherwise have access to professional advice.

There has been much – although perhaps not enough – debate within the profession on the extent to which solicitors are meeting the real needs of their clients, and the extent to which perception of solicitors as part of the service economy is compatible with the elevated sentiments expressed in the Code. Solicitors who attempt to live up to those sentiments should also be painfully aware that financial constraints, for example those of legal aid or recovery of costs in a litigation may indirectly affect their advice or actings and this should be made clear to the client at the time.

Solicitors must exercise their own judgment. In England this has been held to mean that a solicitor must not blindly follow counsel but must 'use his own common sense and form his own opinion'[1]. The court has the option to award costs against a solicitor (or counsel) who has wasted court time and this has been held to include a solicitor who engaged a clearly incompetent counsel[1]. A solicitor employed as the chief legal adviser by a local authority should have direct access to the council and committee of the authority he or she is advising and the same principle applies to all solicitors in the commercial and public sector. Solicitors who act as directors and company secretaries of client companies should be aware of their duties as directors and consider whether these are compatible with the giving of independent advice. The Law Society does not consider it necessary to state as a policy that solicitors should never accept such appointments[2] but solicitors should be aware of the potential for conflict of interest and the effect this

1. *Davy-Chiesman v Davy-Chiesman* [1984] 1 All ER 321.
2. Company Law Committee 1994.

may have. Similar considerations arise if the solicitor is appointed as trustee of a pension fund, particularly in the context of an insolvency where the solicitor will almost certainly have a good working relationship with the insolvency practitioner appointing the independent trustees.

With exceptions for solicitors employed in the public and commercial sector, solicitors who conduct investment business may not be tied exclusively to a particular financial services company and must act independently in respect of all investment transactions[1]. Introductions to a particular financial services company are allowed, provided the firm is satisfied the company product(s) would meet the requirements of the best advice rule.

Many solicitors have close relationships with estate agents and building societies and many instructions will derive from third party recommendations. However, any commissions received from a third party should be disclosed to the client. This is simply an example of the common law rule of agency that an agent may not make a secret profit. More difficult is the issue of what conditions (including restrictions on the level of fees) may be imposed by clients, for example by major banks, as a condition of the solicitor remaining on a nominated panel of solicitors recommended to clients or instructed by the banks. On one view the solicitor-client relationship is a contractual one and the parties are free to negotiate terms, however onerous. Although in so far as conditions imposed may compromise the independence of the solicitor's advice - however difficult that would be to demonstrate – such an arrangement would be unprofessional. The Law Society is likely to issue guidelines in respect of third party referrals, reminding a solicitor that where a client is introduced to a solicitor by a third party in terms of an arrangement between the solicitor and the third party, the solicitor should recognise that the first duty is to the client. The Law Society is considering recommending that the client should be advised by the solicitor in writing at the earliest opportunity that the solicitor is not

---

1. Solicitors (Scotland) (Conduct of Investment Business) Practice Rules, r 3.7.

acting for the third party and that the primary duty of care is to the client. There will also be a specific restriction on the solicitor acting in the purchase of property sold by or through the agency of a third party where the survey has been arranged through a third party. The solicitor will be required to deliver a copy of the account to the client when a VAT invoice is raised. Further guidelines will deal with advertising of solicitors' fees by a third party.

Relations with other professions is considered in chapter 9 but the threat to the independence of the solicitor is one of the reasons why so many European countries (including Scotland) have resisted the idea of multi-disciplinary partnerships.

Provision of professional services

Where earlier emphasis was upon the knowledge and learning of professionals, the emphasis at the time of writing is upon how legal services are provided and the quality of service.

Competence

Competence has always been expected of a solicitor[1] and this obligation to provide adequate professional services is enshrined in the Code of Conduct, rule 5. Incompetence can be breach of contractual and delictual duty and can lead to a claim for professional negligence. This is no more than an expression of the common law position and the same rules should apply in a claim of professional negligence in relation to the burden of proof and remoteness of damage as in any other claim for negligence, although the position of the disappointed beneficiary appears to be an anomalous exception to this general rule[2].

The solicitor is expected to exercise the skill of an ordinary

1. Law Society's Memorandum to the Monopolies Commission 1968, p 4.
2. See pp 92–93.

solicitor exercising reasonable care[1]. A solicitor may be able to claim that he or she is entitled to the same immunity from an action in negligence as an advocate when acting as an advocate in court or performing pre-trial work very closely associated with the case, and this immunity extends to the solicitor advising on a plea. In England it has been held that the immunity may not extend to a solicitor when an advocate is engaged to advise, although it does not necessarily follow that the absence of immunity means that the solicitor is necessarily negligent[2].

A solicitor is not responsible for the fraud or negligence of an auditor as such but might be liable in negligence if there had been a failure in performing due diligence. Solicitors acting for large commercial clients such as property developers often co-ordinate the necessary professional reports and collateral warranties and should take care to ensure that both they and their clients are clear as to the extent of the solicitor's instructions and responsibilities. It may also be prudent to inquire into the level of other professionals' insurance cover, bearing in mind that solicitors' insurance under the Master Policy is perhaps the most comprehensive cover available. A solicitor can be liable to investors where knowingly contravening the Financial Services Act 1986 but ordinarily owes no duty of care to potential investors or shareholders.

At one time the Law Society's policy was that any civil action for negligence had to be pursued before the Complaints Committee could refer a case to the Discipline Tribunal. The view now is that the two can be pursued simultaneously: there has to be a balancing exercise of weighing the public interest in the prompt and efficient operation of the disciplinary scheme as against the risk of prejudice to the fairness of other proceedings. In England it has been held that, where the public interest required that inquiries had to be made by a professional tribunal with a view to the institution of proceedings, it was not in the public interest that those inquiries be stayed until the outcome of the civil actions, involving essentially the same subject matter, where there was no reason to think that the inquiry and any disciplinary measures would not be con-

1. *Hunter v Hanley* 1955 SC 200.
2. *Somasundaram v M Julius Melchior & Co* [1989] 1 All ER 129.

ducted fairly[1]. Proper preparation for the defence on one front will also serve as a defence for another, although the taking of any steps under the 1980 Act, ss 42A(2) or 53A(2) (in respect of inadequate professional service) cannot be founded upon in any proceeedings for the purpose of showing that the solicitor was negligent[2]. A direction to pay compensation for inadequate professional service may be taken into account in the computation of any award of damages in an action for professional negligence[3].

Incompetence

Abject incompetence can also be professional misconduct. This is a question of emphasis. Mere negligence does not itself justify a finding of misconduct; however it may do so. In the words of Lord President Cooper:

'Two criticisms were addressed to us by Counsel ... The first was that professional negligence, however crass, can never amount to professional misconduct, a proposition which [counsel] supported by reference to early English cases. What the law of England was, or is, on that matter I do not know. There is negligence and negligence: and I am certainly not prepared to affirm the proposition that according to Scots law and practice professional negligence cannot amount to professional misconduct.'[4]

A failure to comply with a rule may and not must be treated as professional misconduct, it being essential to consider the whole circumstances and the degree of culpability of the solicitor acting in all the circumstances[5]. The circumstances cannot include ignorance of a new practice rule and solicitors have a duty as well as an interest to be familiar with all the Law Society's rules and regulations. Even the solicitor's condition, such as depression or ill health, does not go to culpability, although it is certainly relevant in mitigation.

Incompetence may justify a finding of inadequate professional service. The 1980 Act, s 42A allows the Law Society to

1. *R v Chance ex p Smith* (1995) Times, 28 January.
2. 1980 Act, s 56A(1).
3. Ibid, s 56A(2).
4. *E v T* 1949 SLT 411.
5. *Sharp v Council of the Law Society of Scotland* 1984 SLT 313.

waive or restrict fees and outlays, and order a solicitor to pay to the client compensation to a maximum of £1,000 for a solicitor's inadequate professional services. The solicitor may also be directed, at his or her own expense, to secure rectification or take any other action in the interests of the client. The 1980 Act, s 65 defines inadequate professional services as 'professional services which are in any respect not of the quality which could be reasonably expected of a competent solicitor'.

A finding of inadequate professional service does not preclude a finding of negligence or misconduct but the terms are not synonymous and the powers under the 1980 Act, ss 42–44 have proved to be of most value in the context of complaints which do not justify litigation or disciplinary proceedings against the solicitor. Typical examples include delay and failure to deal with correspondence and to keep the client informed. While the Tribunal has held it is not necessarily IPS not to attend a hearing where there is no stateable defence, it was IPS for the solicitor not to advise the clients that he would not be attending the hearing, and of his reasons for acting and the potential consequences[1].

Specialists

A solicitor is required to exercise the level of skill appropriate to a particular matter and should not therefore accept instructions where the solicitor considers the service might be inadequate owing to lack of knowledge or experience.

Solicitors are now free to describe themselves as specialists either because they can demonstrate this from experience or because the solicitor is an accredited specialist under the Law Society accreditation scheme. However where a solicitor describes him or herself as a specialist the public is entitled to assume that the solicitor's skill and expertise are greater than the average. Although there have as yet been no awards of IPS against solicitors describing themselves as specialists, it is difficult to resist the argument that 'a competent solicitor' must in this context mean 'a competent specialist solicitor' and that

1. 1993 JLSS 200.

this would be taken into account in assessing the standard of service.

Where a solicitor is unable to demonstrate that the claim to be a specialist is justified, this would be a breach of the Solicitors (Scotland)(Advertising and Promotion) Practice Rules 1991 and may be treated as professional misconduct. It is unlikely that a single act of negligence or IPS would be sufficient to justify a finding that a claim was unwarranted, but the solicitor should be aware that there is the possibility of a finding of both IPS and professional misconduct.

6. Clients' papers and mandates

Ownership

Documents and papers delivered by the client to the solicitor clearly belong to the client. So far as correspondence is concerned, the general rule is that original letters belong to the recipients, so that letters written to the client belong to the client and letters written to third parties belong to them. However, since the solicitor conducts correspondence as agent for the client, original letters to the solicitor from third parties belong to the client, as do copies of the solicitor's own correspondence. Notes of meetings and telephone calls have been held to belong to the solicitor, since it is the professional duty of solicitors to keep such records in the performance of their proper functions[1] and the same reasoning would appear to apply to inter-office memoranda[2]. More problematic may be computer-generated information, for example document tracking programs in a complex commercial litigation or arbitration. These are usually generated by the solicitor but are probably of greater value to the client, at least where the matter in question is not finally concluded. Where the solicitor and client communicate by electronic mail it may also be difficult to categorise the documentation in conventional terms and the Law Society has not yet had to address some of these issues.

The ownership of a precognition rests with the solicitor[3] and the copyright similarly belongs to the solicitor. Precognitions are professional tools to be used in the client's interest, and generally should not be exhibited to third parties. They may be exhibited to third parties or to the client in accordance with the client's instructions if and only if compliance is in accordance

---

1. *Fisher v Fisher* 1952 SC 347 per Lord President Cooper.
2. Opinion of CK Davidson QC for the Council of the Law Society of Scotland November 1982.
3. *Swift v Brannigan* 1991 SCLR 604.

with good professional practice taking into account the whole circumstances of the case[1]. Whether disclosure or exhibition should be made is a matter for the solicitor's professional judgment, but it would be clear for instance that it is not good professional practice to release precognitions simply for their 'entertainment value', whatever the client's specific instructions. The solicitor should also consider the effect which release of precognitions might have upon the conduct of third parties, such as parents of a rape or traffic accident victim, and the extent to which release of information may prejudice further conduct of an action or a police investigation into money laundering[2].

Since the liquidator of a company steps into the shoes of the directors, the liquidator is entitled to any papers or information to which the directors would have been entitled. Similarly the trustee of a bankrupt is entitled to papers and information relating to the bankrupt's financial position, but probably not to papers and information relating to the bankrupt's personal circumstances. Where the property is subject to a charge the title deeds belong to the heritable creditors. Where forwarded to solicitors 'under the usual conditions' this includes a duty on the solicitor not to release them except to another solicitor on a similar undertaking.

Destruction

Since most papers within a solicitor's files are clients' property, strictly speaking the permission of the client is required before these can be destroyed. Clearly where express permission is granted, the solicitor may proceed but in other cases the solicitor may be safe to assume that permission has been granted. There is no reason in principle why express permission should not be incorporated at the outset in a client agreement letter: if not, permission can be sought at the end of a transaction and in some circumstances might be implied, for example from previous discussions.

1. Criminal Law Committee 10.8.1994.
2. See chapter 13.

In 1984 and again in 1990[1] the Law Society issued guidelines suggesting retention periods for different types of action, which range from expiry of the time for appeal in a simple debt collection to ten years after termination of a continuing trust. However in all cases the onus rests with the solicitor as to whether it is safe or prudent to dispose of a file in a particular case. The guidelines relate only to correspondence files: it is suggested that important papers such as confirmations, decrees etc should be kept indefinitely; however given the constraints of storage space it may be preferable that as many as possible are returned to the client on completion. Many documents, for example prior writs and titles returned when land registration is effected, may be of interest to local archives and local archivists are usually pleased to advise whether any items would be of interest for long term deposit. It should be borne in mind that the Money Laundering Regulations now impose a requirement to retain the solicitor's own papers (usually for five years) while the Accounts Rules impose an obligation to retain papers for ten years.

As noted elsewhere[2] the duty of confidentiality extends even after termination of the transaction and/or the agency. Accordingly, the solicitor should ensure that confidentiality is preserved where files are sent for destruction. The safest procedure is probably to shred the files within the office but if a third party is to be involved, the solicitors should satisfy themselves that precautions are taken to preserve confidentiality, for example files should not simply be 'dumped' on public sites.

Effect of mandates

Where the solicitor receives a mandate, that terminates the agency and the normal rule is that the solicitor should not undertake any further work from the date the mandate is received unless there are exceptional circumstances, for example where the mandate is delivered within days of a trial and the client's position would be prejudiced if there were no

---

1. 1984 JLSS 198, 1990 JLSS 206.
2. See p 52.

solicitor acting in the interval before transfer of the agency. The solicitor should obtemper the mandate by delivering the papers belonging to the client (see above). After doing so, the solicitor may raise with the client, in writing, reasonable queries as to why the mandate was obtained but may not delay obtempering the mandate pending a reply from the client[1]. 'Reasonable queries' in this context means that:

'a solicitor might reasonably seek information as to whether or not the client considered that the firm had failed in some way to satisfy the client or if the client had been put off the firm of solicitors in some way, but that it would not be appropriate for the solicitors to invite the former client in any way to resume his original business connection.'[2]

Where solicitors have initially acted for more than one party, such as husband and wife, and continue to act for one, they are entitled to retain the file but should make it available on loan to solicitors subsequently acting for another party to make copies[3].

Where the client is in receipt of legal aid and there is an application for transfer of agency the Scottish Legal Aid Board (SLAB) is required to consider whether there is a good reason for the transfer and if it is still in the interests of justice for the client to continue to receive legal aid in summary cases or in appeal cases. In solemn cases, 'good reason' is the only test and this may include conflict between co-accused, convenience or some act or omission which has led to loss of confidence in the original solicitor. The application is refused where there is no reason or explanation provided. The agreement of the original solicitor is not 'good reason', nor is the original solicitor's consent or opposition a relevant factor to the test although the information which the solicitor provides may well be relevant[4]. If there is any delay in securing the transfer it may be that the client's position is prejudiced, and there are differing views whether in these circumstances the original solicitor should still continue acting in the interim. On the one hand, the client has made it clear that the professional relationship has terminated, and accordingly the solicitor's authority has

---

1. Tribunal decision 636/84.
2. Council Report May 1991.
3. 1986 JLSS 273.
4. SLAB Guidelines.

terminated. On the other hand, whatever the general rule, it can hardly be bad professional practice for a solicitor to act in the client (or former client's) interest, if the interests of justice require this. There may be circumstances to warrant a solicitor continuing to act once a mandate has been received, but these would be exceptional. Unhelpful as this may be, perhaps all one can say is that the response must depend upon the circumstances and the exercise of the solicitor's judgment. However it should be clear that the interests of the accused must come first and the solicitor who continues to act on receipt of a mandate must be in a position to demonstrate that any action was taken in the interests of the accused and not of the solicitor.

Since a precognition is deemed an aide memoire for the solicitor it does not form part of the papers deliverable to the client[1]. However SLAB will not pay for the client to be precognosed twice and as a matter of courtesy the solicitor should deliver precognitions to another solicitor in response to a client's mandate. The solicitor should not deliver precognitions to a client direct.

Obtaining mandates

Obtaining mandates must be within the constraints of the Solicitors (Scotland) (Advertising and Promotion) Practice Rules 1991. A solicitor is not entitled to seek a mandate directly when requested to act for a client by the client's parents or friend: the proper procedure is to suggest to the family friend that the potential client should contact the solicitor. In criminal cases only the duty solicitor is entitled to receive payment from SLAB for the first appearance. No other solicitor is entitled to be present in court without specific instructions and solicitors attending court for a specific client would be acting improperly in making general inquiry of other potential clients.

Where one partner is leaving a practice, ideally the partners should agree on the approach to clients. In the absence of agreement it is not improper for the partner to advise clients if

---

1. *Swift v Brannigan* 1991 SCLR 604.

leaving to practise elsewhere. Despite the fact that a client may view an assistant as his or her solicitor, the solicitor/client relationship technically subsists between the client and the firm. An assistant only undertakes work for the client either on the general or specific instruction of a principal, and so is not entitled to claim a client as an established client[1] or to write directly to former clients offering the services of a different firm[2]. Where the partnership is dissolved, a notice of dissolution is normally sent to the clients who make their own choice of which new firm to engage, either by signing a formal mandate or by personal contact. The production of a list of clients circulated by a former partner is not a professional duty but a matter for agreement between the parties either in a partnership contract or a minute of dissolution[3].

Liens

In principle a solicitor has a general lien over all papers placed in his or her hands by the client to cover the business account and associated fees and outlays. This does not entitle the solicitor to obstruct the course of justice, so papers required for an existing court action must be delivered as soon as reasonably practicable in accordance with a mandate, and immediately if required, for example where there is a pending motion for summary decree. Where the client wished to recover papers in order to raise an action for professional negligence against former solicitors, it was held that the solicitor was entitled to exercise a lien and withhold papers until payment of an outstanding account[4]. Since this case was decided, the introduction of IPS and the revised complaints procedure may mean that the exercise of a lien has lost some of its effectiveness, but is still competent.

If exercising a lien, the solicitor should quantify the account for fees and outlays as soon as possible. Where a solicitor is prepared to relinquish a lien in exchange for a mandate to pay

---

1. Solicitors (Scotland) (Advertising and Promotion) Practice Rules 1991, r 2(1).
2. Council Report, December 1991.
3. Professional Practice Committee 2.12.93.
4. *Yau v Ogilvie & Co* 1985 SLT 91.

an outstanding account at some future date, for example from the proceeds of sale of a house, the solicitor should be aware of the difference in effect between a mandate and an assignation in the event of the client's insolvency[1]. Where client's found caution to cover fees secured by a lien over papers, it was held that a special case existed to warrant the solicitors being ordained to deliver the papers so the clients could instruct other solicitors[2].

1. See 'Mandates, assignations and arrestments' 1993 JLSS 185; 'Mandates and assignations' 1994 JLSS 175.
2. *Boyd v Drummond Robbie & Gibson* 1994 SCLR (Sh Ct) 777.

7. Confidentiality and privilege

Confidentiality and the client

The observance of client confidentiality is a fundamental duty of all solicitors[1]. The solicitor must not disclose any information about the client's affairs, and that duty extends to all staff employed by the solicitor. The duty transmits to the executors of a deceased client, or to any person who stands in place of the client, for example it could be enforced by a curator bonis of an incapax if the solicitor sought to disclose prejudicial information about the incapax.

The duty continues even after the solicitor-client relationship is terminated and a solicitor may not use confidential information about a former client's affairs for the benefit of another client. A solicitor who has acted for husband and wife jointly may not therefore use information as to a party's bank account or the destination of proceeds of sale to intercept funds on behalf of either party individually. In England it has been held that although there was no general rule that a firm who had acted for a former client could never act for another client against a former client, a firm could not so act where a reasonable man would reasonably anticipate that there was a danger that confidential information gained while acting for a former client might be used for the benefit of the new client. The erection of 'Chinese walls' and physical separation of both documentation and staff was not sufficient to overcome the risk[2]. Since Scottish solicitors have the same duty of confidentiality, the same principles should apply and solicitors should be at the least very wary when instructed to act against former clients.

These issues arise acutely in the context of the merger of solicitors' firms, and even the very substantial costs of

1. Code of Conduct, r 4; see also the Data Protection Act 1984.
2. *Re a firm of solicitors* [1992] 1 All ER 353.

're-educating' new solicitors and the loss of personal experience may not outweigh possible prejudice[1]. The costs and possible loss of clients must be one of the disadvantages to be taken into account in assessing the virtues or otherwise of a merger.

Confidentiality may be waived by the client, for example the client may authorise the solicitor to use the client's name in an advertisement. In that case, the client's name or business may be identified in an advertisement, but only with the prior written consent of the client[2]. The client's consent is also required to television broadcasting, although not to traditional court reporting. Where the solicitor is acting under a continuing power of attorney or as guardian ad litem, the solicitor necessarily has to disclose details about the client's affairs and it must be assumed that the appointment itself confers a general consent to disclosure, although presumably only for the purposes of conducting the client's affairs.

However even where the client waives confidentiality, it may not always be proper professional conduct for the solicitor to disclose the information. It is difficult to strike a balance between disclosure in the client's interest and discretion in the interests of justice: there has been relatively little experience and therefore consideration in Scotland of the type of ongoing publicity familiar in the American court system, but there is undoubtedly a trend towards solicitors giving public interviews about ongoing cases (usually criminal or compensation cases). At some point disclosure and discussion of the client's position may become sufficiently partial and visible to infringe on the solicitor's duties to the court and to the profession. If the solicitor is seen as bringing the profession into disrepute, that may be professional misconduct, regardless of whether or not the solicitor was acting on the client's instructions in publicising the client's predicament. It would almost certainly be professional misconduct for the solicitor to sell his or her memoirs in respect of a sensational case contemporaneously, although as a matter of professional conduct no exception is taken to autobiographies etc which are not contemporaneous.

1. *Supasave Retail Ltd v Coward Chance* [1991] 1 All ER 668.
2. Solicitors (Scotland) (Advertising and Promotion Practice) Rules 1991, r 8(5).

Confidentiality and third parties: privilege

It has long been accepted that legal privilege attaches to certain communications between the solicitor and client, and that the solicitor is not obliged to breach the duty of confidentiality to the prejudice of the client. This may seem at odds with the solicitor's duties to the court, but it is recognised that without the benefit of privilege the administration of justice would be difficult if not impossible, and the individual client's interests therefore coincide with the public interest in the proper administration of justice.

The general rule was stated by Lord Emslie:

'as far as we can discover from the authorities the only circumstances in which the general rule will be superceded is where fraud or some other illegal act is alleged against a party and where the law agent has been directly concerned in the carrying out of the very transaction which is the subject matter of the inquiry.'[1]

The solicitor is not therefore obliged to disclose information or release client's papers without authority from the client. Although it is good professional practice for the solicitor to cooperate with the police as far as possible, if the solicitor is requested to give a statement to the police or fiscal investigating the affairs of a client, the solicitor should first take instructions from the client. In respect of matters which the solicitor considers are confidential, the solicitor should request that he or she be precognosed on oath before the sheriff. The solicitor should seek guidance from the sheriff in respect of any question the answer to which might be a breach of confidentiality. Similarly the solicitor should not deliver documents to the police nor allow a search without production of a search warrant. If the solicitor has received no prior notice of the application for a warrant, it may be appropriate to contact the fiscal and inquire why there has been no hearing. It should be borne in mind that no party is entitled to a 'fishing expedition', whether by way of search warrant or specification, although there is clearly a measure of discretion and speed may be of the essence in a criminal action or, for example, in proceedings for breach of copyright. If served with a specification of docu-

---

1. *Micosta SA v Shetland Islands Council* 1983 SLT 483.

ments, the solicitor indicates the existence of any documents which are thought to be privileged and lodges these in an envelope marked 'Confidential': admission of those documents is a matter for the court[1].

A solicitor can always ask to take a precognition from another solicitor but the original solicitor cannot breach confidentiality in relation to the client in a precognition. A solicitor can be cited as a witness and the court then rules on the question of confidentiality if the matter arose[2]. Where correspondence between solicitors is marked 'without prejudice' the assumption is that it cannot be founded upon to the prejudice of the writer's client. However if privilege is at issue, the court may examine the document and allow it to be founded upon if satisfied that it is not entitled to privilege[3]. Where the client waived privilege by founding upon correspondence with his solicitor, it was held that he had waived privilege in respect of all relevant correspondence[4] and there is of course no privilege where the client calls the solicitor as a witness.

'It is considered essential to the proper preparation of a party's case that he may insist that any material communications relating to that preparation should be protected against disclosure to the court. Similarly a broad privilege attaches to communications between a party and his professional legal adviser.[5]'

The question of privilege has arisen almost exclusively in relation to the court: although conceivably it may also arise in non-contentious matters, such as in the execution of due diligence or in planning matters, and solicitor/client communications are privileged although they may not relate to any specific legal proceedings actual or contemplated[6]. The communications must however be associated with the giving of advice[7]. In England it has been said that the test 'is whether the communication or other document was made confidentially for the purpose of legal advice. Those purposes have to be construed broadly[8]'. It is doubted if firms can obtain protection for their

1. The context of the *Micosta* decision.
2. Professional Practice Committee 6.12.1990.
3. *Watson-Towers v McPhail* 1986 SLT 617.
4. *Wylie v Wylie* 1967 SLT (Notes) 9.
5. I D McPhail 'Evidence' 10 *Stair Memorial Encyclopaedia* para 681.
6. 10 *Stair Memorial Encyclopaedia* para 682.
7. *Balabel v Air India* [1988] 2 All ER 246 (CA).
8. *Balabel v Air India* [1988] 2 All ER 246 at 254 per Taylor LJ.

records merely by depositing them with a solicitor: the matter 'must have formed part of the substance of the original seeking or giving of legal advice and not have an independent origin'[1]. However in England the courts have been reluctant to distinguish between information which is given to the solicitor by a third party, and that which passes directly between solicitor and client[2]: all information in the hands of the solicitor in connection with the matter is entitled to privilege. It may be that, even when the solicitor subsequently declines to act, a duty of confidentiality and possibly the special protection of privilege can be created[3] but there is no privilege where the existence of the solicitor-client relationship is at issue[4].

On the basis of older authorities, privilege is said not to attach to legal advice from unqualified persons although it may apply where the client has a bona fide belief that the person was duly qualified[5]. However, the structure of solicitors' firms has now radically altered and, since the duty of confidentiality extends to all within the solicitor's firm, the writer suggests that privilege should also extend to any working within the firm, for example trainees, paralegals or in-house accountants who act on instructions from the solicitor, irrespective of whether the client is aware of their status. To rule otherwise is to place the client, and indeed the firm, in an invidious position; for example is financial advice on marital breakdown privileged if given by the first year solicitor but not if given by the qualified accountant employed by the firm? Where communication is made to someone not in their capacity as a qualifed lawyer it is said that no privilege attaches even where the person happens to be qualified, for example legal advice given by CABX advisers or academic lawyers (although the client is entitled to insist on confidentiality)[6].

Disclosures to ACAS are expressly protected from disclosure to the industrial tribunal[7] but it is less certain that there is

---

1. Wilkinson *The Scottish Law of Evidence* (1986) p 94.
2. *Re Sarah C Getty Trust* [1985] 2 All ER 809.
3. R Black 'A question of confidence' 1982 27 JLSS 299. See also *Minter v Priest* [1930] AC 558.
4. 10 *Stair Memorial Encyclopaedia* para 682.
5. G Maher 'Professional privilege' 1990 JLSS 108.
6. Maher, above.
7. Employment Protection (Consolidation) Act 1978, s 133.

privilege for disclosures made to those acting as conciliators. There is probably no privilege where the custody or welfare of a child is at issue[1]. Where a dispute has been referred to alternative dispute resolution (ADR), the parties expressly agree that discussions are confidential and a plea of personal bar might be taken if one party attempted to breach this agreement in subsequent proceedings. If the Civil Evidence (Family Mediation) (Scotland) Bill becomes law in 1995, as seems likely, there will be statutory privilege for certain evidence revealed in mediation proceedings.

Exceptions to the rule

There is no confidentiality, and thus no privilege, if it is alleged that the communications were made 'in the furtherance of any criminal purpose', for example to obtain advice on the commission of a crime, whether or not the solicitor was aware of the client's purpose. This should be distinguished from communications made after the commission of the crime for the purpose of obtaining advice on the defence to a criminal charge or communications made for the purpose of obtaining advice whether or not such a proposed course of action is lawful, where communications are privileged[2]. With the multiplicity of criminal sanctions for commercial actings, such as insider dealing, this distinction may occasionally be difficult to draw.

Another exception to the rule of confidentiality is the decision that prison authorities may read and censor letters concerning potential legal proceedings between solicitor and client[3]. Lord McCluskey ruled that the prisoner's right to reasonable facilities for private consultation was sufficient to fulfil the requirement that the prisoner be permitted effective and unconditional opportunity of seeking confidential advice by practical means. His view was that the rule of confidentiality applies essentially to the procedure for recovery of documents

---

1. 10 *Stair Memorial Encyclopaedia* para 684.
2. *Wilkinson* p 97.
3. *Leech v Secretary of State for Scotland* 1993 SLT 365.

incidental to the conduct of some litigation and that 'it is in no sense a basic civil right for all purposes'[1].

There may also be statutory powers which require the solicitor to breach the duty of confidentiality, particularly in relation to drug trafficking and money laundering[2]. Documents should be delivered in response to a search warrant or court order (although only those covered by the warrant or order)[3] and disclosure may also be required in the context of an investigation by the European Commission into infringement of article 85 or by the Director General of Fair Trading[4]. Under the Solicitors (Scotland) Accounts Rules 1995 solicitors may be required to produce books and other documents relating to a client's affairs for the inspection of a professional accountant appointed by the Law Society and may also be required to produce information to the Society under the Professional Indemnity Insurance Rules. The solicitor's duty of confidentiality is overriden by the duty to obey the law and 'in particular to comply with the rules made under the authority of statute for the conduct of the profession'[5]. It may also be argued that the client impliedly consents to inspection by/as instructed by the Law Society in the context of the client's expectation not only that the solicitor will comply with these professional rules but also that the solicitor will provide an adequate professional service.

In examinations in bankruptcy, no privilege attaches to communications between the solicitor and client. Where companies are concerned, the solicitor acting as an insolvency practitioner is obliged to deliver transcripts of examinations carried out under the Insolvency Act 1986, s 236 if served with a notice by the Serious Fraud Office, except where the transcripts are the subject of legal professional privilege. The court has discretion to decide what is covered by privilege: in the forceful words of Lord Browne-Wilkinson:

'the extraction of private and confidential information under compulsion from a witness otherwise than in the course of inter-partes litigation is an

---

1. 1993 SLT 365 at 372E
2. See chapter 13.
3. *VDU Installations Ltd v Integrated Computers & Cybernetics Ltd* (1988) Times, 13 August.
4. Solicitors (Scotland) Act 1980, s 64C.
5. *Parry-Jones v Law Society of England and Wales* [1968] 1 All ER 177, (CA).

exorbitant power. It is right that such information should not be generally available but should only be used for the purposes for which the power was conferred. Although, as will appear, in my view there are severe limitations on the way in which such a discretion can be exercised where prosecuting authorities are involved, it is important that no doubt should be cast on the discretion of the court to decide who shall have access to such information.'

Nevertheless, the extent to which implied confidentiality and public interest immunity attaches to all transcripts of examinations is debatable and the insolvency practioner may be required to deliver these even after an assurance of confidentiality has been given in the context of a voluntary interview².

Different concepts of confidentiality and privilege

Although the CCBE Code recognises the duty of confidentiality for all solicitors, it should be noted that courts of each member state interpret confidentiality differently. In some jurisdictions, the obligation of confidence is owed only to the client: in others, such as France, it is considered *d'ordre publique*, so waiver by the client is not enough. The lawyer retains the discretion as to whether confidentiality should be waived. In England, much of the law of confidentiality has developed in the context of general discovery in civil proceedings to which there is no exact equivalent in Scotland, although it is likely that Scottish courts would derive considerable assistance from English authorities, particularly in relation to commercial and corporate issues.

In Scotland, there is no distinction between the position of the solicitor in private practice and the in-house lawyer: the latter is subject to the same obligations and duties, including the duty of confidentiality and the employee is presumably therefore entitled to invoke privilege. The position is different in different member states; for example it is broadly similar in

---

1. *Re Arrows (no 4)* [1994] 3 WLR 656.
2. See *Re Barlow Clowes Gilt Managers Ltd* [1992] Ch 208; see also *Re Arrows (no 4)* [1994] 3 WLR 656.

Germany, but not in France[1]. The European Commission has ruled that there is no privilege attaching to communications between in-house counsel and their employers[2] and has in fact used advice of in-house lawyers as evidence against the employers[3]. However the *AM&S* decision has been much criticised as out of date and may not survive scrutiny by the European Court of Justice[4].

1. P Marchandise 'The confidentiality of the company lawyer' in 'New liabilities and challenges for industry in Europe': Proceedings of 5th European Conference of Company Lawyers 1994.
2. *A M & S v EC Commission* [1982] ECR 1575.
3. *John Deere* OJ L035/58 14.12.84; *Sabena-London European* OJ L317/47 4.11.88.
4. See also *Saunders v UK* (Sept 30 1994, unreported) European Court of Human Rights.

8. Conflict of interest

Common law rule

The common law rule is that a solicitor may not act for two parties where their interests conflict or where there is a serious possibility that a conflict may arise. The rationale for this rule can be found in the nature of the agency relationship of a solicitor to the principal. Agency is fiduciary relationship and the agent must at all times act in the interest of the principal.

At its most obvious, a solicitor may not act for both pursuer and defender in a civil action, or for the prosecution and defence in a criminal action. There the parties' interests are so clearly seen to conflict that the solicitor cannot conceivably discharge his or her professional duty to both clients. However, there are many other occasions where the interest of the parties may conflict. The situation where the solicitor acts for both vendor and purchaser in a transaction, or for both borrower and lender has given rise to very considerable debate and intervention by the Law Society in the form of rules and guidelines but there are also other less obvious examples, such as a solicitor acting for husband and wife, for a partnership and the individual partners; or for a company and the individual directors.

The critical test is whether the solicitor can adequately discharge all duties to his or her respective clients equally. It has been suggested that to act for parties with conflicting interests is objectionable: 'not only does the agent incur a double liability, but difficulties arise with regard to delivery of fees so prepared, the right of lien over them, and the respective responsibilities of the parties to the acts of their common agents[1]'.

Perhaps even more critical is the question of confidentiality.

1. Begg *Law Agents* (2nd edn) p 337.

If matters are in the public domain or common to both parties, there may be no conflict, for example company accounts, partnership accounts, memorandum and articles of the company, existing shareholders' agreement. However, information passing between a solicitor and client is in principle confidential[1]. It follows that where facts disclosed to a solicitor on behalf of one client which may be prejudicial if disclosed to another client without the authority of the first, there is almost certainly a conflict of interest. This may include information which the solicitor has obtained, for example from examination of titles, and may even extend to matters in the public domain where there is a difference in emphasis or interpretation, such as as the extent of a director's authority. Although the doctrine of constructive notice may not extend to banks acting as principals[2] it seems clear that it does extend to knowledge acquired by the solicitor, who acts as agent for the clients not as a principal. In one graphic example, *Chapelcroft Limited v Inverdon Egg Producers Ltd*[3] the solicitors acted for both parties: the solicitors' knowledge as agent was imported to their principal and accordingly the principal could not succeed in an action for reduction of a Minute of Agreement and repayment of the purchase price where the seller had no title to the subjects. There was no suggestion of intention to deceive and in the circumstances the principal was bound by his agent's knowledge. The position is different where there is fraud by the agent: an innocent principal is not liable for an agent's fraud unless committed within the scope of the agent's authority or unless the principal has obtained some gratuitous benefit at the expense of a third party as a result of that fraud[4].

It can be argued that there is no conflict of interest where disclosure is made equally to both clients, for example where the solicitor does a full report on title and leaves both borrower and lender to make a commercial decision as to whether any defects in title are acceptable. The interests of purchaser and borrower it is argued are identical in the sense that they both require a valid marketable title, and where both parties accept

1. *Micosta v Shetland Islands Council* 1983 SLT 483, and see chapter 7.
2. *Mumford v Bank of Scotland, Smith v Bank of Scotland* 1994 SLT 1288.
3. 1973 SLT (Notes) 37 OH; see also *Thomson v MB Trustees Ltd* 1994 GWD 32-1894.
4. *McCabe v Skipton Building Society* 1994 SLT 1272.

the position there is no conflict. However this is far too simplistic, as discussion in relation to commercial transactions (see below) shows. In considering the New Zealand case of *Clark Boyce v Mouat*[1], the Privy Council held that there was no general rule of law that a solicitor should never act for both parties in a transaction where their interests might conflict. The position was summarised by Lord Jauncey[2] as:

'rather is the position that he may act provided he has obtained the informed consent of both to his acting. Informed consent means consent given in the knowledge that there is a conflict between the parties and that as a result the solicitor may be disabled from disclosing to each party the full knowledge which he possesses as to the transaction or may be disabled from giving advice to one party which conflicts with the interest of the others.'

While it might be correct that a solicitor can continue to act with informed consent, it would be most unusual for the parties to agree that the solicitor is disabled from giving advice. Most clients and indeed most solicitors would see it as an essential part of their duty to the client to give advice. Certainly at the point where their solicitor is asked to give advice and comment and it is reasonably foreseeable that the client will act upon this advice and comment, the difficulties of non-disclosure become apparent and even silence or refusal to comment may in some circumstances be construed as advice or comment. Moreover, in proffering meaningful advice it is hard to see how a solicitor can resist preferring the position of one client to another[3].

The decision of whether or not there is a conflict of interest is one for the solicitor's own judgment. In the view of the Discipline Tribunal 'it is only the solicitor himself who can have all the information upon which a decision can be made', an observation which highlights the fact that the critical issue is one of information. The Tribunal is perhaps too sanguine in its view that 'if the solicitor is in doubt, it is a straightforward matter for him to arrange for one of the parties to be separately advised'[4]. In some situations it may be difficult to suggest to

1. [1993] 4 All ER 268.
2. [1993] 4 All ER 268 at 273.
3. See also *Farrington v McBride & Partners* [1985] NZLR 38.
4. Annual Report of the Discipline Tribunal 1993, p 3.

clients that they must seek independent legal advice as *Clark Boyce v Mouat* showed[1]. It is a common criticism of divorce proceedings that the involvement of lawyers only exacerbates an already difficult situation. Equally, potential shareholders who are about to set up a new company and enter into a shareholders' agreement may see it as unnecessary to incur additional expense of separate representation. However, it is not the client's perception which is the deciding factor, but that of the solicitor. Regardless of informed consent, the test is ultimately an objective one, in that where a solicitor has acted in a case where there is a conflict of interest, this is a breach of rules amounting to professional misconduct and attracting significant penalties in the event of a claim for negligence. Moreover, it should be borne in mind that, in construing conflict of interest, 'the solicitor' means the solicitor's firm. It is not permissible for different solicitors in the same firm to act for persons who have a conflict: the rule catches all solicitors within the firm[2].

Solicitors (Scotland) Practice Rules 1986

The Solicitors (Scotland) Practice Rules 1986 which came into effect on 1 January 1987 create a more formal regulatory framework in relation to conveyancing transactions. Some have argued that there should be an absolute prohibition against acting for both parties, but at present the Rules indicate situations in which a solicitor may act. However this is always subject to the overriding proposition set out in rule 3 'a solicitor shall not act for two or more parties whose interest conflict'.

In terms of rule 5 a firm of solicitors cannot act at any stage for both seller and purchaser in the sale or purchase or conveyance of heritable property, or for both landlord and tenant, or assignor and assignee in a lease of heritable property for value or for a lender and borrower in a loan secured over heritable property. However where no dispute arises or might reasonably be expected to arise between the parties and (other

---

1. [1993] 4 All ER 268; see also *Forster v Outred & Co* [1982] 2 All ER 753.
2. *Cleland v Morrison* (1878) 6 R 156, adopted by the Discipline Tribunal and approved in Tribunal decision 689/86.

than in exception (a)) the seller or landlord of residential property is not a builder or developer, this rule is not to apply to certain specified situations. The exceptions are:

(a) the parties are associated companies, public authorities, public bodies or government departments or agencies; or
(b) the parties are connected with one another within the meaning of the Income and Corporation Taxes Act 1970; or
(c) the parties are related by blood, adoption or marriage, one to the other, or the purchaser, tenant or assignee or borrower is so related to an established client; or
(d) both parties are established clients or the prospective purchaser, tenant, assignee or borrower is an established client; or
(e) there is no other solicitor in the vicinity whom the claimant could reasonably be expected to consult; or
(f) in the case of a loan to be secured over heritable property, the terms of the loan have been agreed between the parties before the solicitor has been instructed to act for the lender, and the granting of the security is only to give effect to such an agreement.

The exceptions set out in rule 5 (1) deal principally with the situation where the prospective clients are closely related by blood, marriage or are deemed to be connected for taxation purposes or are established clients. However, even where that close association exists, the solicitor may only act for both parties where the seller or landlord is a builder or developer if the solicitor has obtained an express waiver from the Law Society. It is the status of the developer and not the property in question which is critical in determining whether a waiver is granted[1] and it is clear that the Law Society will only grant a waiver on good cause shown. If there is any doubt, the Law Society will always exercise prudence and refuse the application even in a situation where that may cause financial hardship. Requests for waivers have fallen into four categories:

(1) A person who is by trade a builder or developer selling in the course of business houses or plots which are part of a larger development.

---

1. Tribunal decision 861/93.

(2) A person who is by trade a builder or developer selling a site or house as a single unit and not as part of a larger development.

(3) A person who is not by trade a builder or developer selling individual plots or houses which are part of a larger development being undertaken by that person.

In all these cases the sellers have the status – whether permanent or temporary – of a builder / developer / a solicitor and require a waiver to act.

(4) A person who is not by trade a builder or developer selling a single plot or site. It had been argued that if planning permission were granted for the site, the seller is regarded as a builder / developer but it is now accepted that a seller in these circumstances is not regarded as a builder / developer and no waiver is required, subject to the overriding proviso that there is no conflict of interest, which remains a matter of judgment for the solicitor[1].

The solicitor is obliged, where exception (c), (d) or (e) in rule 5 (1) applies, to advise both parties at the earliest opportunity that he or she, or the firm, has been asked to act for both parties, and that if a dispute arises they or one of them would have to consult an independent solicitor. This must be confirmed in writing immediately, as must the fact that a document sent for signature may have legal consequences and the client should seek independent legal advice. Meanwhile the exceptions stated in rule 5(1)(f) have to a large extent been overtaken by the debate in relation to commercial transactions, considered below.

For the purposes of rules 4 and 5, a solicitor shall, unless the contrary is proved, be presumed to be acting for a party for whom he or she prepares an offer whether complete or not, in connection with a transaction of any kind specified in the Rules, for execution by that party. Acting for a potential purchaser in connection with mortgage or life insurance advice has been held to be acting at a stage[2]. A solicitor acting as an estate agent – even in cases where all offers were to be submitted to another firm of solicitors who would be doing the conveyancing – is acting at a stage and rule 5 applies[3] . Although a

1. Council Report October 1994.
2. Professional Practice Committee 5.5.94.
3. Professional Practice Committee 4.11.93.

solicitor may take advantage of the established client exception[1] both clients or the prospective purchaser must already be established clients and advantage cannot be taken of the exemption if the solicitor-client relationship has only been established with one of the parties before commencement of the transaction. However, a solicitor, or a firm, may act on behalf of two or more prospective purchasers or tenants provided that the clients are informed of that intention. This would permit the firm to, for example, submit competing offers for domestic property or a retail unit in a large development. The rule is that a solicitor must, of course, keep details of the price, any other terms of the offer and any other advice confidential to the respective client. The rule goes on to reaffirm the proposition that a single solicitor shall not, when he or she has given any advice to one of the clients with respect to the price or rent to be offered, or with respect to any material condition of the prospective bargain, give advice to another of the clients in respect of such matters, which raises the question whether the solicitor is giving an adequate professional service to the second client. Whilst therefore it is technically possible for a single solicitor to submit competing offers, it is difficult in practice to see how the solicitor would not in so doing be either in breach of duty of confidentiality to one client or duty to render an adequate professional service to the other.

Commercial transactions

The issue of conflict of interest in commercial security transactions was the subject of significant debate in late 1993/94. With effect from 1 November 1993, claims against the Master Policy for Professional Indemnity Insurance have attracted 'double deductibles' or excesses where there has been a breach of the conflict of interest rules. Against that background, the Scottish clearing banks reiterated their view that 'there is scope for conflict of interest to arise in preparation of security for almost every commercial advance'[2]. Aware that the Society's insurers

1. Rule 5(1)(d).
2. Letter from A W A Scott, Secretary to the Committee of Scottish Clearing Banks DLSS November 1993.

would likely be looking much more closely for any hint of conflict of interest, the banks identified a need for both solicitors and banks to adjust their practices in relation to the preparation of securities for commercial advances, which in many cases would mean a requirement for independent legal advice. After consultation with the Committee of Scottish Clearing Banks, the Law Society was able to issue guidelines for commercial security transactions which the Society has defined as one which 'relates to the secured lending to a customer of a Bank or other lending institution where the purpose of the loan is clearly for the customer's business purposes'[1]. The guidelines are reproduced as Appendix 1 and illustrate some of the instances where lenders and borrowers might have separate interests in commercial security transactions.

The Scottish banks have now introduced a policy of instructing separate solicitors to represent them in major transactions, although the banks have reserved the right to instruct the borrower's solicitor to act for them in de minimis cases. Bearing in mind that the maximum excess which a partnership might face if a claim arises is currently limited to £40,000 and bearing in mind also that the bank faces a risk that, if it does not act responsibly by employing separate solicitors, this may be regarded as contributory negligence, the Royal Bank of Scotland, for instance, has decided that de minimis cases should be restricted to those instances where the borrowing secured or to be secured does not exceed £40,000. Having said that the bank reserves the right even in de minimis cases to seek separate representation when this is considered appropriate. Conversely, the bank may instruct the same solicitors even where the loan is in excess of £40,000 and this may be acceptable if the loan is for a specific purpose and restricted to specific securities. Where the loan is to secure indebtedness of a trading company by floating charge, standard security, cross guarantees, covenants and deposit of other securities and covenants, it is very doubtful that the same solicitor should act for the bank and borrower whatever the borrowing limit. The banks have made it clear that the borrower is still expected to meet all legal fees and outlays in respect of a transaction, and

1. Letter from President of the Law Society, 15.2.1994, reproduced as Appendix 1.

the borrower would undoubtedly prefer that one solicitor should act, thereby minimising costs. However as stressed earlier, the ultimate decision is one for the solicitor, bearing in mind the terms of rules 3 and 5(1)(f) referred to above.

Husband and wife

Care must be taken when acting for husband and wife since their interests may not always coincide. Even where there are no known matrimonial difficulties at the time the parties consult a solicitor, spouses may have very different interests. Perhaps the most likely situation is where a wife is asked to sign a standard security over the matrimonial home in respect of the husband's business debts. Both parties should be made fully aware of the extent of the security which is being granted. In particular it should be drawn to the wife's attention that an 'all sums due' clause may mean that additional loans will give rise to further secured borrowings without her being obliged to sign additional documentation. Although the English courts have taken the view that the banks have a duty in these circumstances to advise the wife of her position[1], the Scottish courts have held that the banks have no such duty (although to fail to so advise would now be in breach of the banking codes of the major lending banks)[2]. However there is no doubt that a solicitor acting for the husband and wife does have a duty in these circumstances to advise the wife that she almost certainly has a different interest from her husband, particularly where there are children who require adequate accommodation for the foreseeable future. The interest to preserve her share of the matrimonial home in the event of a business failure may be diametrically opposed to the interests of the husband, let alone those of the lending bank. The solicitor should therefore be certain to advise the wife of her right to seek independent legal advice, and at the very least should be writing to the wife separately, not by way of a single letter addressed to husband and

1. *Barclays Bank plc v O'Brien* [1994] 1 AC 180.
2. *Mumford v Bank of Scotland, Smith v Bank of Scotland* 1995 SLT 1288; but see also *McCabe v Skipton Building Society* 1994 SLT 1272.

wife. However the best advice in these circumstances is undoubtedly to insist that the wife consults another solicitor. If the wife does not do so, a letter in terms of the Practice Rules 1986, rule 7 must be sent with the standard security.

Other situations where the interests of husband and wife may not be identical are where they are entering into partnership together or where they are to become shareholders in a private limited company. It is not at all uncommon for the wife to have a minority shareholding and to be a designated director and/or company secretary. If the company is an 'off the shelf' company and there is no special protection for minority shareholders, the wife may be in a very vulnerable position both as regards the value of the shareholding and potential liability for wrongful trading. It is quite proper for the solicitor to act for both parties in such a situation, but the potential drawbacks of the minority shareholders' position should be clearly identified to them at the outset and they must always be free to seek independent advice. Since a partnership can mean unlimited joint and several liability, extreme care should be taken before advising a husband and wife to form a partnership which may put at risk the entire matrimonial assets. Given the increasing number of divorces, remarriages and complex family relationships, it is also unwise for a solicitor to assume that husband and wife wish their whole estate to fall to the other automatically and specific instructions should be obtained on whether any disposition should contain a survivorship clause.

Where there are known matrimonial difficulties, it is even more dangerous for the solicitor to act for both parties. In *Worth v Worth*[1] the parties reached an agreement between themselves and, although advised to take independent advice and seen separately by the solicitor, insisted on one solicitor acting. When the wife attempted to have the agreement set aside, alleging conflict of interest, the sheriff held there was no substance in the conflict argument 'where the financial interests do not conflict'. The Law Society considers that it is for the solicitor to judge whether a conflict exists, not for the clients[2], and a solicitor acting is always subject to the overriding nature

1. 1993 GWD 2666.
2. 1994 JLSS 67.

of the Practice Rules 1986, rule 3. The solicitor is aware that very different considerations may apply to husband and wife, particularly where there are children and there is a possibility that the Child Support Agency may be involved at a later date, or where there are substantial pension rights or capital assets. The solicitor should try and seek a legally binding agreement dealing with all financial aspects including what is to happen to the proceeds of the matrimonial home. If this is agreed, the solicitor may act for both parties in the sale of the matrimonial home. However where there is no formal agreement the solicitor should not act in the sale. Note that an agreement to place the proceeds on joint deposit pending resolution of the dispute between the parties would be a binding agreement in terms of the guideline and the solicitor could act in the sale[1], although solicitors should consider whether it is in the client's best interests to have the whole proceeds tied up on joint deposit for what may be a considerable period of time.

Acting for relatives

As has been stressed elsewhere, the solicitor has a duty to know the client. Where a solicitor is instructed on behalf of an elderly relative, the solicitor must be quite clear of the extent to which the relative is acting as agent and the extent to which the parties interests do or do not coincide. Where 'the family' are assisting with a purchase, the solicitor should consider the interests of the lenders. Is (say) the title to be in name of the parents but the loan to be secured over the property? If it is, the parents should be aware of the potential risks if they default on any agreed repayment terms and the potential for family disagreement. If the loan is not to be secured, the lender's position should be considered. It is not sufficient to rely on a will as protecting the interests of a lender, since a testator is always entitled to change a will and legal rights do not apply to heritable property.

---

1. 1994 JLSS 146.

Where one member of a family is selling to another, the price may be at issue but it would be inappropriate for a solicitor to advise on this and where there is any doubt about this or any of the terms one of the parties must be advised to seek separate legal advice. Where a parent is granting a guarantee in security of a family member's indebtedness, the same principles in relation to independent advice apply as with husband and wife. Although the solicitor acting for both mother and son in *Clark Boyce v Mouat*[1] was found not liable in negligence, in very similar circumstances it was held that the solicitor in *Forster v Outred & Co*[2] would have been liable in negligence had the claim not been time-barred.

Executries

Where there is conflict between a solicitor/executor and other executors as to whether the solicitor's firm should continue to wind up the estate, the solicitor/executor should not use his or her position to secure that the firm continues to act. In such circumstances, the solicitor has a discretion either to cease acting or to resign as executor; if the solicitor ceases to act but remains as executor he or she should confer with the executors to see which other firm should take over administration of the estate. Failure to do so places the solicitor in a conflict of interest between the role as executor and the personal interests of the solicitor. If the solicitor resigns as executor, he should obtemper a mandate if the executors resolve that another firm should act. The decision however is one for the executors, and not for the beneficiaries[3].

It is a well-established principle that a solicitor may not take instructions to act in the preparation of a will which contains a significant benefit to that solicitor, his or her family or any partners or their family. There would be a conflict of interest and the solicitor would be open to a claim that there had been

---

1. [1993] 4 All ER 268.
2. [1982] 2 All ER 753.
3. 1986 JLSS 248.

duress or undue influence. In these circumstances the client should instruct a solicitor from another firm who should take instructions, advise the testator, prepare the deed and have this executed. This has been held to apply even in the preparation of a codicil which diminishes the testamentary benefit to a solicitor, since even in preparing a codicil, it is a solicitor's duty to review the prior testamentary writings. In taking instructions for a codicil the proposed variations cannot be viewed in isolation and it is necessary for the solicitor to advise the testator in relation to the whole testamentary provisions[1].

Recognised exceptions to this general rule permit the solicitor to make a will for his or her spouse, parents or children, or perhaps collaterals on the understanding that any potential beneficiary is not materially disadvantaged. The solicitor may also include a specific bequest of a small item or small legacy from the estate[2]. In one of the few recent reported cases, the Tribunal strongly disapproved a solicitor acting in preparation of a will in which he was left share of residue of one-seventh, although in all the circumstances of the case the Tribunal did not find professional misconduct[3].

Partners and partnerships

Liability for partnership debts is joint and several: where the parties are exactly equal partners it may be that there is no potential conflict of interest and it is therefore appropriate for a solicitor to act for all parties, say in preparing a partnership agreement. However even where the parties are equal, there are implications, for example in provision for majority decision making which should be spelt out to the parties and may make it appropriate that they should seek independent advice. It would certainly be questionable for a solicitor to act in drawing up a deed of admission for a new partner without being certain that the partner had the opportunity to seek independent advice on the extent of the liabilities which were being

1. Tribunal decision 699/87.
2. 1989 JLSS 389.
3. Tribunal decision 755/89.

assumed. It is an interesting question whether that duty extends to admitting a new partner to the solicitor's own partnership: it is surprising how little inquiry some solicitors appear to undertake on their own behalf but in the absence of fraud or breach of warranty the rule here is presumably *caveat emptor*.

Directors and shareholders

In small private companies it may be difficult to differentiate between the interests of shareholders and directors, and between the duties owed by a director to the company as such and his or her own interests. As with partnerships, individual shareholders who are entering into a shareholders' agreement should be advised of their separate interests and it should be clear which solicitor is then acting for the company, for example in relation to any bank borrowing and floating charge. If shareholder/directors are to grant personal guarantees, clearly they may have contrary interests and where shareholder/directors are making loans to the company, the terms of any ranking agreement may be contentious. The terms of any share option or indeed the length of any service contract may also be at issue.

Where the company is trading profitably, there are unlikely to be too many difficulties arising out of the director's relationship with the company itself. The Companies Act 1985, s 320 requires all directors to declare their interests, which allows directors to vote on contracts in which they have an interest, so if notice is given, the solicitor may rely on this when acting for the company and the directors (although shareholders' approval may be required under s 320 even for an arms-length transaction). Directors should be aware at the time of appointment of the circumstances in which they may be removed from office and clearly the solicitor cannot continue to act for both the company and a director who is in dispute with the company, whether because of unfair dismissal or otherwise.

The Companies Act 1985, s 35B presents a particular dilemma: while this section provides that the validity of an act done by a company shall not be called into question on the grounds of lack of capacity in the company's memorandum, and the parties to a transaction have no duty to inquire as to the capacity of the company or authority of the directors, it is still the duty of directors to observe any limitation on their powers and seek ratification by special resolution where appropriate. This may place the solicitor acting for both bank and borrower in a difficult situation if examination of the memorandum discloses any fundamental flaw.

Where the company is in financial difficulties the solicitor advising the board should make the directors aware of the potential consequences of wrongful trading for the directors as individuals, as well as for the company. It may well be that the solicitor who is advising the board should advise the directors to seek independent legal advice on their position, although the parties may be reluctant to do this not least because of the cost, which will not be met by the company. There is almost certainly an inherent conflict of interest between the directors where proceedings are instituted for wrongful or fraudulent trading. The conflict of interest between the directors may be particularly severe if any of them have significant share options or shareholdings or have outstanding loan accounts. For larger public companies there are additional issues of corporate governance and compliance with stock exchange codes etc which lie outside the scope of this work but which may affect the relationship of the directors to the company.

Insurers and the insured

Solicitors are frequently instructed by insurers to pursue a claim in the name of the insured by virtue of their subrogated rights under an insurance policy. Although the policy may allow insurers to nominate solicitors and instructions are initially from insurers, the insured have an interest in any proceedings to the extent that there is a deductible or excess under the policy which the insured have to meet. In some cases this may be considerable. The insured may also wish to pursue a claim for losses, for example loss of profits which were never covered by the policy and in some cases the uninsured losses may exceed the sum insured. Although it is quite proper for the solicitor to act, care should be taken that different interests do not become conflicting interests. Both parties should be quite clear for instance in what proportions they are to meet costs if the claim is unsuccessful and what should be done if the parties cannot agree to accept advice on a settlement.

Where the insured are the defenders, the solicitor's position may also be complicated by the defenders' perception of damage to their reputation, which may be critical to the insured but of less interest to the insurers. In all these cases it is far better for one party to be separately advised than to feel at best that there has been undue pressure to accept an unattractive settlement, at worst that the solicitor has not acted in their best interests.

Criminal cases

A solicitor may properly be instructed to act for several co-accused but the possession of confidential information may be critical. A solicitor may not accept instructions from both where acting for one co-accused might lead to breach of the duty of confidentiality to the other. Where a solicitor took instructions from two brothers charged with different offences in respect of different incidents, it was not acceptable for the solicitor to continue acting for both where one brother's defence was that the other had committed the crime[1]. In *Saminadhen v Kahn*[2] it was held that it would be improper for a solicitor who had acted for one defender to subsequently act for a co-defender.

Difficult situations may also arise where a solicitor is instructed by the directors of a company which is being investigated by the police or Serious Fraud Office. Under the Companies Acts the director or secretary of a company may be liable to default fines and other penalties. In addition a director

1. Tribunal decision 809/90.
2. [1992] 1 All ER 963.

may incur personal liability under the Insolvency Act 1986 and, as noted above, there is likely to be an inherent conflict of interest between directors who are a party to any such proceedings or to an application under the Company Directors Disqualification Act 1986.

The position of the solicitor

The Code of Conduct and the Solicitor (Scotland) Practice Rules 1986 are quite clear. The solicitor may not act where there is a conflict of interest, and where the solicitor does so, he or she is likely to be found guilty of professional misconduct. In 1986 the Discipline Tribunal was of the view that ' many solicitors still seem to be unaware of the serious consequences of continuing to act in a conflict of interest situation and the considerable current public concern on this aspect of professional practice by solicitors'[1]. Nearly a decade later it is highly unlikely, and certainly inexcusable, that any solicitor is still unaware of the serious view which the Society and the Tribunal take of a solicitor acting where there is a conflict of interest.

Quite apart from the fact that breach of the Rules may be followed by disciplinary proceedings, it should also be borne in mind that any claims on the solicitors' professional indemnity insurance arising from acting after 1 November 1993 in breach of rules 3 and 5(2) of the Solicitors (Scotland) Practice Rules 1986 attracts a double deductible. The firm will also suffer the usual penalty loading. This double deductible was imposed as part of the Society's risk management initiative, aimed at reducing claims on the Master Policy by heightening solicitors' awareness of certain danger areas. It has been followed by a series of Road Shows for the profession, and personal letters from the President of the Society and from the insurance brokers stressing the financial penalties which inevitably follow from a claim where there has been a conflict of interest.

The solicitor should have in place a system which enables the firm to identify potential conflicts of interest. Where the firm

1. Tribunal decision 689/86.

considers it may legitimately act, the basis on which the solicitor has reached the decision should be documented on file and, where appropriate, a letter should be sent to both parties. Where the transaction is one between builder and developer, the written waiver from the Law Society must also be retained.

Where the solicitor considers that a conflict of interest has arisen, the solicitor should only continue acting for one party in preference to another if the solicitor has the written consent of both parties, since the solicitor would otherwise almost certainly be in breach of the duty of confidentiality to the client who was invited to seek advice elsewhere. It would be highly unlikely for any new solicitor to advise such a client to consent to the previous solicitor continuing to act in circumstances where, by definition, the previous solicitor has information which may be prejudicial to the new client. As a general rule therefore, the solicitor is prevented from acting for either client where a conflict of interest has arisen. As noted earlier, the solicitor should be sufficiently well prepared and sufficiently alive to the possibility of conflict of interest that it should not be necessary to advise a client only at the last minute that separate representation is required, say one week before the proof. It should be borne in mind that if a solicitor withdraws from acting in the middle of a transaction this may prejudice the client's position. The prejudice is not simply in the inconvenience and tangible costs of, say, instructing new solicitors and delay in completion, but in the less tangible loss of 'intellectual property' and even market perception, since the abrupt change may be seen to prejudice the client's position. It may also prejudice the solicitor's position to be seen as lacking judgment and / or practice management in making an initial assessment. Unless there are exceptional circumstances, the client who is so advised may legitimately ask whether the solicitor has been adequately prepared and has provided an adequate professional service up to that point.

In construing conflict of interest it is clear that 'the solicitor' means the solicitor's firm. It is not permissible for different solicitors within the same firm to act for parties who have a conflict: the rule catches all solicitors within the firm[1]. Bearing

---

1. *Cleland v Morrison* (1878) 6 R 156, adopted by the Discipline Tribunal and approved in Tribunal decision 689 / 86.

in mind that the duty not to act in a conflict arises from the confidential nature of the solicitor-client relationship, it is not surprising to find that it has been held that there may be a conflict
of interest, in the sense that there may be a breach of confidentiality, between successive clients. In England it has been held
that the erection of 'Chinese walls' may not be sufficient to prevent a firm from acting against a former client, where 'it is reasonable to anticipate that there is a danger that information
gained by the firm while acting for the former client may be
used against him'[1]. For the same reason, the solicitor may not
subsequently accept instructions from one party to arrest
funds where the information as to the whereabouts of the
funds arose out of acting for the arrestee, for example from acting for husband and wife jointly or acting for company and
directors/shareholders. The same considerations apply to the
use of information arising out of commercial negotiations –
having advised a landlord when entering into a commercial
lease, can the solicitor subsequently act for the tenant knowing
not only of the landlord's personal circumstances but also
weaknesses in the covenants or irritancy clause?

It is not uncommon for a solicitor to find that in acting for
one client A, a contentious issue may arise in relation to client
B for whom the solicitor would normally act – and indeed may
be acting in a number of other current transactions, but not
hitherto in this transaction. In these circumstances, although
client B is an established client, the solicitor may not (at least in
the absence of a formal retainer from client B) abruptly terminate the relationship with client A simply because client B is a
better economic prospect. A solicitor has a duty to client A
which should not be overriden by an economic relationship
with client B. Conversely, client A cannot expect the solicitor to
automatically terminate the relationship with client B, simply
because client A is now on the scene. There is a difficult balance
to be struck, but in these circumstances it would seem not
unreasonable to rely on 'Chinese walls' provided all the parties
are satisfied that the necessary relationship of trust between
the solicitor and the client can be maintained.

---

1. Re a firm of solicitors NLJ 31 May, 1991. See also *Saminadhen v Kahn* [1992] 1 All
   ER 963.

9. Relationship with third parties

Whereas it is possible to analyse the relationship of the solicitor and client almost exclusively in terms of the agency relationship, the position of the solicitor in relation to third parties certainly derives from more abstract notions of professional and befitting conduct, and from a duty to act in the public interest.

Duties to the court

The Scottish solicitor is regarded as an officer of the court. Although every practising solicitor is required to be a member of the Law Society, a person is only formally admitted as a solicitor after the Council or the individual has presented a formal petition to the court, which makes the order of admission[1].

As an officer of the court, the solicitor 'must never knowingly give false or misleading information to the court and must maintain due respect and courtesy towards the court while honourably pursuing the interests of their clients'[2]. In presenting a case or facts in mitigation, the solicitor (including fiscals who are officers of the court both in right of being fiscals and as solicitors) must not give any information which the solicitor knows to be incorrect. The solicitor should not allow a witness to give perjured evidence, although there may well be inconsistencies in evidence. The solicitor is bound to ensure the court is referred to all the relevant legal authorities whether or not those authorities support the solicitor's argument (attempting of course to distinguish those which are not in the client's favour)[3]. In presenting a case before the commercial court in the Court of Session, the solicitor is now entitled to assume that the judge has read the pleadings and familiarised

1. Solicitors (Scotland) Act 1980, s 6.
2. Code of Conduct, r 8.
3. *Glebe Sugar Refining Co v Greenock Harbour Trustees* 1921 SC (HL) 72; Code of Conduct, r 8.

himself with the facts and documents lodged, while both parties will have exchanged written statements and notes of argument, if relevant, before any procedural hearing. The judge also has a more interventionist role at the preliminary and procedural hearings. The main purpose of these hearings is 'to achieve a speedy resolution of cases,...to reduce to a minimum the time spent preparing cases for proof or debate, and the time spent in court on proof or debate, proving or arguing points which at the end of the day turn out to be immaterial'[1]. Accordingly, parties must be fully prepared for the preliminary and procedural hearings and it must follow that solicitors have a duty to the court as well as their clients to be so prepared. The same duties apply to the solicitor when acting in the sheriff court: for example, the solicitor must adequately prepare for an options hearing and a continuation of an options hearing is only allowed on cause shown[2].

Where two cases are scheduled in different courts for the same day it is the solicitor's responsibility to make arrangements to ensure that each client is separately represented. It may be contempt of court and professional misconduct to fail to appear on behalf of a client or to ensure that another solicitor and/or counsel appears. There is generally no objection to solicitors operating a 'pool' for routine attendances at court, but the solicitor appearing should have adequate instructions in each case. The writer's view is that there is a dual responsibility since the solicitor appearing as agent has an obligation as officer of the court, while the instructing solicitor is liable as the principal to ensure that the agent has adequate instructions. Some sheriffs have taken the view that only the principal agent may appear at an options hearing, which can be distinguished from an intermediate diet where there is no obligation to answer.

The duty to the court is not limited to court appearances but also extends to procedural matters. Thus before raising an action, the solicitor should have undertaken reasonable investigation and thereafter should proceed without delay. It is not unprofessional to raise an action without investigation if there is a prima facie case and the danger of missing a time limit: however it would be unprofessional to wilfully delay the

---

1. N Morrison 'Scotland's new commercial court' 1994 JLSS 354.
2. Act of Sederunt, Ordinary Cause Rules 1993, SI 1993/1956, r 9.12.

issue of court proceedings until the last minute because there is a prospect of settlement and a larger fee. The lodging of skeleton defences should be avoided except in cases of extreme urgency[1] although it must be recognised that the 7-day (as opposed to previous 14-day) rule puts considerable pressure on those acting for defenders[2]. It is unprofessional conduct to abuse the court process by seeking continued further unjustified adjustment periods: indeed, if these are necessary because of the solicitor's own delay in precognosing witnesses etc, this could also amount to inadequate professional services. In commercial causes the court has the power to find the solicitor liable in any expenses caused by delay if a document is not lodged within the necessary time limit[3]. The ultimate sanction is decree in favour of the other party, although this is used only rarely, but other sanctions may include a refusal of leave to lead witnesses where a list of witnesses had not been lodged under the optional procedure[4]. It may also be both unprofessional conduct and inadequate professional service to so delay preparations that the solicitor has not seriously explored the possibility of settlement (including ADR) well before proof stage: certainly constant settlement at the door of the court does not necessarily denote a well-ordered practice or due respect and courtesy to the court, clients or third party witnesses.

There are signs that the emphasis on standards of service and efficient conduct of litigation is seen to have an application beyond the role of solicitors to all those involved in the judicial process: in England (although not yet in Scotland) it is not unknown for barristers to be found liable for wasted costs, while in Scotland a landmark decision at first instance, although dismissed on appeal, has led to an ex gratia payment of parties' costs by the Scottish Courts Administration when a continued diet of proof was discharged owing to the unavailability of the sheriff[5]. It is the declared intention of the government that judicial costs, including judicial salaries, should be

1. 1986 JLSS 248.
2. Act of Sederunt, Rules of the Court of Session 1994, SI 1994/1443.
3. RC 1994, r 47.16.
4. *McGunnigal v D B Marshall (Newbridge) Ltd* 1993 SLT 769; and see Morrison, above
5. *Meekison v Uniroyal Englebert Tyres Ltd* 1995 JLSS 85.

met out of court fees paid by litigants[1]. How this is to be recon-
ciled with the solicitor's duty to the court or the concept of
judicial independence is unclear. If this approach is taken to its
logical conclusion it may be argued that the users of the service, who are paying for it, are to be entitled to stipulate the
performance indicators, to require particular standards of service and to seek appropriate remedies from all participants if
those standards are not met. The concept of inadequate professional service is one with which solicitors are familiar but the
concept of a direct contractual or delictual nexus between the
judge and the litigant is, to say the least, alarming.

In the context of litigation there is not normally any duty of
care to the opponent, as it is accepted this would cause
grounds for endless litigation. In England it has been held that
the solicitor is under a duty to the court and to a party who is
not legally aided, to the extent that the solicitor must not take
advantage of the fact that the client is legally aided and not
liable to pay costs, for example by prolonging the litigation in
order to force an otherwise unwarranted offer in settlement[2].
However this is a matter of degree: there will always be a nuisance or settlement value in any case, if only because of the
management time and resources which have to be devoted to
fighting any claim, however unjustified. In Scotland the position is exacerbated by the gulf between judicial costs recoverable and actual solicitor-client costs.

The solicitor has a duty to conduct litigation so as not to take
unfair advantage of the fact that a client is legally aided: there
may also be a duty not to take advantage of the fact that a pursuer may require to repay benefits to the Compensation
Recovery Unit[3] although it may be argued that the solicitor is
entitled to use all legal means to protect a client's position.

Difficult issues also arise in relation to arrestments: the general rule is that pursuers are entitled to use arrestment and
inhibition in security of a claim and solicitors have a duty to
consider whether to seek security on behalf of a client.
Pursuers are not liable in damages if they have proceeded regularly, even though the claim is ultimately unfounded, unless

---

1. Hansard Report of the Committee on Statutory Instruments of 9 February 1994.
2. *Kelly v London Transport Executive* [1982] 2 All ER 842.
3. For examples see F Maguire 'Compensation recovery' 1994 JLSS 455.

there has been a defect in the warrant or execution or the diligence was executed with malice and want of probable cause. While the underlying principle is that litigants should not be deterred from taking advantage of their legal remedies[1], it is entirely foreseeable that the laying of an arrestment will disrupt the commercial operations and reputation of the defender and of third parties, for example another shipowner or cargo interests even if it is later conceded that the arrestment was not successful. The writer suggests that the solicitor has at least a duty to consider the effect of an arrestment on a potentially innocent third party, and that it is not good professional practice for a solicitor to instruct arrestment without making reasonable inquiries, for example by inspection of public registers as to ownership of a vessel[2]. It is also irresponsible to instruct arrestment without being in a position to take immediate instructions from clients where it should be envisaged that recall would be sought by the defenders, for example immediately before a long holiday period.

Witnesses

In the course of an investigation the solicitor must not do or say anything which could affect evidence or induce a witness, a party to an action or an accused person to do otherwise than give in evidence a truthful and honest statement of that person's recollections.

If citing witnesses, the solicitor should give as much notice as possible and should attempt to minimise inconvenience for all witnesses. Although attempts are usually made to accommodate engagements of expert witnesses, all witnesses are entitled to equal consideration. The witness should be advised of the position with regard to expenses as soon as possible. Although there is no absolute rule that no witness should be cited without first obtaining a precognition, the solicitor (particularly where acting under a legal aid certificate) should not cite witnesses unnecessarily, bearing in mind both potential inconvenience to the witnesses and cost to the public purse. If

1. *Notman v Commercial Bank of Scotland* 1938 SC 522 at 532.
2. For detailed discussion see 'Diligence on the Dependence and Admiralty Arrestments' (Scot Law Com Discussion Paper no 84).

personally cited as a witness the solicitor is bound to appear, but is bound to observe the duty of confidentiality in so far as protected by privilege[1].

Counsel

In the past it was said that where the solicitor instructed counsel, the solicitor was entitled to rely on counsel: indeed Lord President Inglis in 1878 was of the opinion that:

'But above all in importance, as affecting the present question, is the undoubted special rule that when the conduct of a cause is in the hands of counsel, the agent is bound to act according to his directions, and will not be answerable to his client for what he does bona fide in obedience to such directions.[2]'

The case concerned a claim for damages by a client who averred that the case had been conducted in breach of his instructions: nowadays it is more likely that the solicitor would be held not liable because there had been a novus actus and it would be impossible to prove causation[3].

Certainly no solicitor or advocate would now regard the solicitor as bound to 'obey' counsel's directions. Indeed the Court of Appeal has expressly stated that 'the solicitor's duty is not just to pass on any views expressed by counsel; he has to consider for himself . . . to use his own common sense and to form his own opinion, although obviously in doing that he will take the view expressed by counsel into account'[4]. The relationship nowadays is much closer to a partnership or joint venture in which each party is bound to discharge specific duties to the client and the court. In the solicitor's case this includes the instruction of competent counsel and in England it has been held that where the solicitor instructed and continued to instruct manifestly incompetent counsel, the solicitor was liable. Conversely it is the solicitor's duty to adequately instruct counsel: this includes applying one's mind to the issues and to the relevant documentation in framing

1. See chapter 7.
2. *Batchelor v Pattison and Mackersy* (1876) 3 R 914.
3. *Somasundaram v M Julius Melchior & Co* [1989] 1 All ER 129.
4. *Davy-Chiesman v Davy-Chiesman* [1984] 1 All ER 321 at 335 per Dillon LJ.

instructions. Whether those instructions are by way of formal memorial or E-mail is a matter of preference: what is important is that counsel is in a position to make an informed judgment. Ideally the relationship between solicitor and advocate effectively combines the different talents of two partners who contribute equally.

Having instructed counsel, the solicitor has a professional duty to meet counsel's fees irrespective of whether the solicitor has received payment. Exceptions are where the client is legally aided or where counsel has undertaken to act on a speculative basis.

Solicitor-advocates

The Law Reform (Miscellaneous Provisions) (Scotland) Act 1990, s 24 made provision for extension of rights of audience to members of any professional or other body on application to the Lord President and the Secretary of State. The Law Society of Scotland has made application and is a recognised body for this purpose, and solicitors wishing to exercise rights of audience in the higher courts may apply through the Law Society to become 'solicitor-advocates'. In order to qualify, the solicitor requires to undergo additional practical and theoretical training, to pass an exam, to subscribe to a supplementary Code of Conduct[1] and to comply with rules for order of precedence, instructions and representation[2].

So far as the court is concerned, the duties of the solicitor-advocate in relation to matters of law are to draw to the attention of the court any previous decision binding on the court or statutory provision relevant to a point of law, whether or not it supports the argument or has been referred to by the opponent. This is probably no different from the duty already owed by any solicitor appearing before the court (it is perhaps worth bearing in mind that because of the extensive jurisdiction of the sheriff courts, Scottish solicitors have traditionally exercised rather greater rights of audience before the lower

1. Code of Conduct (Scotland) Practice Rules 1992, Sch 2.
2. Solicitors (Scotland) Order of Precedence, Instruction and Representation Rules 1992.

courts than their colleagues in England). The solicitor-advocate accepts personal responsibility to the court for any pleadings which he or she signs and should not sign pleadings drafted by someone else unless in exceptional circumstances.

At the time of admission of the first solicitor-advocates concerns were expressed as to whether they would find that their duties to the court as advocates might in any way conflict with their role as solicitors. The supplementary Code sets out express duties in both criminal and civil cases particularly in relation to how far the solicitor may proceed with an action or a plea, although none of these conflict with the ordinary rules of professional ethics for solicitors. However in some areas there are differences. For instance, the Law Reform (Miscellaneous Provisions) (Scotland) Act 1990 and subsequent regulations enshrine for solicitor-advocates what has long been the position of advocates in relation to the cab-rank rule and precedence of instructions. Solicitor-advocates are not subject to the cab-rank rule, by which any advocate is required to be available (on the instructions of the Dean of Faculty if necessary) to take over an action on behalf of a colleague otherwise instructed. In the case of the solicitor-advocates, where instructions have been accepted, the Secretary of the Law Society exercises the same power as the Dean where there is a conflict and may require another solicitor-advocate to take over conduct of a case. While handing over a case as instructed by the Secretary would not therefore be professional misconduct, the aggrieved client might well argue that he or she had received an inadequate professional service. This reinforces the need for any solicitor, including the solicitor-advocate, to run an efficient and well-managed office, where last-minute changes can be accommodated without prejudice or inconvenience to the client.

One area which caused initial difficulties is in the instruction of junior counsel. The Dean of the Faculty ruled against 'mixed doubles' in the sense of a solicitor-advocate and advocate appearing together in any court, whether civil or criminal, on the basis that rules of ethics and practice are so different as to cause difficulties. As more solicitor-advocates are admitted this may be less of a problem as it will be as practicable to field a team of solicitor-advocates as advocates.

Another issue is whether solicitor-advocates are or are not subject to the rule that advocates should not see witnesses, apart from expert witnesses. The supplementary Code provides that there is no general rule that a solicitor-advocate may not discuss a case with a potential witness, but when instructed by a solicitor the solicitor-advocate is entitled to insist that instructions are accepted on the basis that the solicitor-advocate will not do so. Practitioners in jurisdictions where there is no separate Bar find it hard to understand how the acting counsel can argue a case properly without a detailed knowledge of the witnesses, preparation etc. Those who have grown up with a separate Bar argue strongly in favour of an independence which gives an ability to focus on the crucial issues without being distracted by administrative detail. Undoubtedly there are arguments both for and against the independent Bar and its distinct rules of ethics and practice. However as advocates are increasingly prepared to accept direct instructions from non-solicitors, it may prove anomalous that they should retain their distance from witnesses, at least in non-criminal matters.

Direct instructions also mean an increasing acceptance of the concept of professional negligence. Both advocate and solicitor-advocate undoubtedly enjoy immunity from damages in respect of court appearances and pre-trial work closely connected with the conduct of the case in court[1]. However when acting in a purely advisory capacity, immunity is not available. It may be that drawing this distinction in the event that a client is dissatisfied with the outcome is what will cause most difficulty for solicitor-advocates in practice.

Meanwhile any solicitor (not merely a solicitor-advocate) identifying a situation which may require appearance in court is bound to advise the client of the advantages and disadvantages of instructing appearance by a solicitor-advocate and counsel respectively[2]. Complexity, cost and relative experience are listed as matters for consideration but in order to comply with the generality of the rule, solicitors should also be aware of the relevant ongoing debates.

---

1. *Saif Ali v Sydney Mitchell & Co* [1980] AC 198, [1978] 3 All ER 1033, HL.
2. Code of Conduct (Scotland) Practice Rules 1992, r 3.

Quasi-judicial bodies

There has been relatively little debate on how far the solicitor's duties as an officer of the court extend to the increasing number of administrative and quasi-judicial bodies. In some cases what started off as relatively informal bodies have over time acquired many of the procedural characteristics of courts, for example planning inquiries. On the other hand, these bodies may have very different rules, for example as to the leading of evidence and the criteria for consideration in, say, childrens panels. The Code of Conduct for Scottish Solicitors simply refers to 'courts' whereas the CCBE Code refers to 'courts and tribunals' and extends the rules governing the lawyer's relationship with the courts to 'his relations with arbitrators and any other persons exercising judicial or quasi-judicial functions'.

It is particularly difficult to say how far the specific duties as officer of the court apply to other bodies where they have an investigative function, for example the Monopolies and Mergers Commission, or the European Commission. This is particularly so as lawyers deal with cross-border transactions, where concepts may be differently interpreted (for example the notion of confidentiality). While it is generally accepted that the lawyer has a duty not to assist the client in breaking the law, it is hard to see (as has been argued) that this concept can preclude a lawyer advising whether or not a transaction is for instance in breach of competition law. Clients are entitled to plan their affairs to best advantage within the law: the difference between tax evasion and tax avoidance. The European Court has accepted that advice as to the effect competition law would have on UK pricing policies would be privileged, even though the only common ground within the member states is that privilege extends only to a right of defence[1].

For the client, the decision of a tribunal is as important as any traditional court. Moreover the fact that these decisions are subject to judicial review reinforces the argument that the solicitor should owe the same duties to tribunals as to the courts. It is probably going too far to suggest that the solicitor owes exactly the same duties to an interventionist body such

1. *A M & S Europe Ltd v EC Commission* [1983] 1 All ER 705.

as the European Commission but even if the duties are not so extensive, it seems to be generally accepted that the solicitor should not deliberately mislead the tribunal and must observe professional standards of courtesy and behaviour generally. Ultimately the solicitor cannot depart too far from the accepted norms, since there is the long stop that any behaviour which may bring the profession into disrepute can constitute professional misconduct.

Notaries public

Although it is a condition of admission as a notary public that the applicant is first a solicitor, the office or profession of notary public is distinct from that of solicitor. The distinction was perhaps more evident before 1992, when the duties and responsibilities of the office of Clerk to the Admission of Notaries Public were transferred to the Council of the Law Society of Scotland[1]. It is still competent for any qualified person to seek admission as a solicitor and not as a notary but a petition for admission as a solicitor may now include an application for admission as a notary. When granting the petition for admission, the court directs the Council to enrol the petitioner as a notary and administer the oath of office as a notary public and register the applicant's name in the Register of Notaries. The oath can be administered by Council members or Council representatives who are themselves admitted as notaries public, although a Council member or representative should not administer the oath to a partner or employee of his or her own firm. The oath which is sworn is 'I will faithfully discharge the duties of notary public in Scotland according to the law'.

The notary originally had a monopoly in relation to the preparation and execution of various deeds, particularly in relation to land transfers and until recording of deeds was introduced in 1617 the notaries' protocol books were the only record of land transactions. The principle that notarial involvement provides authentication of a deed survives more clearly in European jurisdictions, but the shadow remains in Scotland.

---

1. The Law Reform (Miscellaneous Provisions) (Scotland) Act 1990, s 37 which came into force on 20 July 1992.

Notaries are routinely required to witness affidavits for the purposes of the Matrimonial Homes Act 1983 and in foreign proceedings and, less commonly, may be required to note a protest against the dishonour of a Bill of Exchange or note a maritime protest against bad weather or incident at sea. The notary may also be required to authenticate the signature or execution of documents for use in a foreign court.

Since the purpose of the notary's subscription is that the document authenticated is indeed the document it bears to be, the notary must take particular care in the authentication. It is therefore professional misconduct to simply alter the terms of a document without reference to the person swearing the deed, to send a document for signature to a client without witnessing the signature or to ask a client to swear to a blank document. Where the notary is effecting notarial execution of a deed on behalf of a party who is not able to personally subscribe, the whole deed should be read out verbatim.

Where the notary has any interest in the deed, this can render the whole invalid, for example where the notary is appointed a trustee under the deed[1] or a solicitor in a trust has the power to charge fees[2]. It may be that this rule is modified so that the deed is invalid only to the extent that it confers a benefit in money or money's worth on the notary: the granter may be able to waive the requirement that the deed is read over[3].

Duties to third parties

A solicitor may be held to owe a duty of care to a third party on the normal delictual principles. As summarised by Lord Jauncey in *Midland Bank plc v Cameron, Thom, Peterkin & Duncans*[4] four factors are relevant to a determination of the question whether a solicitor while acting for a client owes a duty of care to a third party. These are:

---

1. *Ferrie v Ferrie's Trustees* (1863) 1 M 291.
2. *Newstead v Dansken* 1918 1 SLT 136, OH.
3. Requirements of Writing (Scotland) Act 1995, (which comes into force on 1 August 1995) s 3(1) and Sch 3, para 2.
4. 1988 SLT 611.

(1) The solicitor must assume responsibility for advice or information furnished to the third party.
(2) The solicitor must let it be known to the third party expressly or impliedly that he or she claims, by reason of his or her calling, to have the requisite skill and knowledge to give the advice or furnish the information.
(3) The third party must have relied upon that advice or information as a matter for which the solicitor has assumed personal responsibility.
(4) The solicitor must have been aware that the third party was likely to so rely.

Merely transmitting information on the client's instructions does not amount to an assumption of responsibility and an instruction to prepare a standard security cannot of itself import a duty to verify the value of the security subjects[1]. However a solicitor is certainly at risk in granting an unqualified certificate of title, just as an accountant and auditor may owe a duty of care to a takeover bidder if he or she approves a statement which confirms the accuracy of accounts which he or she has previously audited[2]. Solicitors may properly be requested by client companies to provide auditors with confirmation of contingent liabilities, but when the Law Society of England and Wales considered the ambit of auditors' inquiries they recommended that solicitors should take care in framing responses to ensure that they do not assume undue responsibility[3].

Beneficiaries

Despite the normal delictual principles, there is judicial authority in Scotland for the proposition that the solicitor who is negligent in the preparation of a will cannot be held liable to a prospective beneficiary who is thereby deprived of a legacy[4].

1. *Midland Bank plc* 1988 SLT 611. But see 'Conflict of interest', chapter 8.
2. *Morgan Crucible Co plc v Hill Samuel Bank Ltd* [1990] 3 All ER 330 ; *Galoo Ltd v Bright Grahame Murray* [1995] 1 All ER at 36 per Glidewell J.
3. 'Information by solicitors for company audit purposes' Law Society's Gazette, August 1970, p 507.
4. *Robertson v Fleming* (1861) 4 Macq 167; *Weir v J M Hodge & Son* 1990 SLT 266; see also *MacDougall v Clydesdale Bank Trs* 1993 SCLR 832, OH.

The rule has been much criticised and it is generally accepted that it is completely at odds with the development of the modern law of negligence, at least where there is any reliance by a third party on the solicitor's actings or representations. In principle it is hard to see why a beneficiary who relies upon a representation by a solicitor and thereby suffers loss cannot claim against a solicitor whereas a bank, building society or any other third party could do so in appropriate circumstances.

There is usually no contractual claim which can be advanced by the executors, as the estate has not suffered any loss. However if it can be proved that the testator intended a particular result which has not transpired owing to the solicitors failure, one would have thought this should in principle be sufficient to found a *jus quaesitum tertio*. In England it has been accepted that such a claim is effectively in a class of its own, and the fact that there is no other remedy available to the disappointed legatee is sufficient to found a right of action[1]. It is inconceivable that this anomaly can continue indefinitely and certain that the position in Scotland will eventually be brought into line with other jurisdictions[2].

Meanwhile there is no doubt that failure to carry out a client's instructions is an inadequate professional service. Since a disappointed beneficiary may well be a person 'with an interest' this raises the interesting possibility of a claim under the 1980 Act, s 42 offering a remedy which the courts cannot afford, although that was never the intention of the section[3].

There is no obligation for a solicitor/executor to account to beneficiaries by way of account, reckoning and payment since this remedy is founded on the (non-existent) relationship of principal and agent[4]. However there is a duty on a solicitor/executor to intimate to potential legal rights claimants that they have a claim, so far as reasonably practicable. If a claim is intimated an executor is personally liable if sufficient funds were not retained in the estate to meet the claim[5].

---

1. *Ross v Caunters* [1980] Ch 297; *White v Jones* [1993] 3 All ER 481.
2. For extension of delictual remedies see *Spring v Guardian Assurance* [1994] 3 All ER 129.
3. See pp 146–147.
4. *Loretto School v McAndrew & Jenkins* 1992 SLT 615.
5. Professional Practice Committee 6.9.90.

There is a duty on an executor or trustee to act as a prudent man of business would. This includes not simply a duty to wind up an estate without undue delay, but to manage the affairs of the trust or executry as a prudent man of business would. There is accordingly a duty to review investment and, in appropriate circumstances, to exercise voting rights. The cost of attending meetings and/or voting has to be offset against the effect on the holding, for example of variation of class rights or excessive directors' remuneration packages. The issue of global custody is assuming greater importance and in some jurisdictions the exercise of voting rights by trustees and custodians may be mandatory.

Scottish Legal Aid Board

Current government thinking is that legal aid should not be demand led and that the government as the funder is entitled to impose funding conditions on solicitors who receive payment via the Scottish Legal Aid Board. To some extent this has been the position for some time, but this approach has gathered pace in the 1990s. The contractual relationship with funders cuts across the solicitor-client relationship and creates tensions which are not always easy to resolve. It is hard for solicitors to accept that restrictions on funding may mean they cannot carry out work for clients to the standard that solicitors and clients would expect, a particular difficulty with civil as opposed to criminal work. The Law Society 's view is that the legally-aided client is entitled to an adequate professional service, and that the same professional standards of courtesy and competence apply, but it would be foolish to pretend that a solicitor can offer the legally-aided client anything approaching the level of service required by large commercial clients. It is also a matter of concern that legal aid is not available for the growing number of tribunals before which clients must appear to vindicate their rights.

The details of the legal aid and legal advice and assistance schemes are outside the scope of this book, but in the context of professional practice it should be noted that the solicitor may not claim payment for advice and assistance given to the client so as to exceed authorised limits without the prior approval of SLAB[1] and accounts should be checked before submission to SLAB to ensure that the account does not include expenses incurred before legal advice or legal aid was granted[2]. The solicitor has a duty to SLAB to advise of any change in the client's circumstances and the client waives confidentiality for this purpose. The solicitor also has a duty to SLAB to see that the legal aid fund is not unduly diminished by prolonging litigation unnecessarily or raising an action where a claim had already been settled (which is unprofessional conduct in itself, whether or not SLAB was involved)[3].

Professional colleagues

Solicitors have a duty to act in a manner consistent with persons having mutual trust and confidence and must not knowingly mislead colleagues or go back on their word, once given[4]. There must be an intention to mislead: it would not be professional misconduct for the solicitor to wrongly state a proposition in law. However a professional colleague is entitled to rely on a solicitor acting in accordance with accepted good practice.

In commercial negotiations each solicitor has a duty to attempt to secure the best possible position for the client. Given each solicitor's duty to render an adequate professional service, it seems to follow that the solicitor is entitled to assume that the solicitor on the other side is competent, has thought through his or her position and intends the effect of any proposed revision. However where it is obvious that a colleague has made an error, for example in omitting a page of a document, it is not good practice to take advantage of this, although it is sometimes difficult to draw the line between flexing commercial muscle and taking undue advantage.

A solicitor has a duty not to make use of information sent to him or her by mistake (for example by fax) and breach of that

1. *Drummond & Co v SLAB* 1992 SLT 337, HL.
2. Complaints Committee A 12.1.1995.
3. *Blyth v Wilson* 1987 SLT 616.
4. Code of Conduct, r 9.

duty may be professional misconduct[1]. If a solicitor receives papers in error, the correct procedure is to return these to the other solicitor unopened.

Missives

There is no duty on a solicitor to ensure that finance is available before submitting an offer but it is good practice to advise the client of the risks in concluding missives without being certain that finance is available[2]. The seller's agent has no duty to advise potential purchasers' agents of the existence of or number of other notes of interest[3] or to fix a closing date where there has been more than one note of interest.

Solicitors and others in Scotland have long maintained that the system of conveyancing, or more particularly the fixing of the closing date and speed of conclusion of missives, is superior to the English system of extensive inquiries before contract and the purchasing 'chain'. The Council of the Law Society takes the view that the closing date system has been successful and in order for that success to continue, all parties should adhere to the same practices. The Law Society guidelines on closing dates therefore require a solicitor to decline to accept instructions to submit a revised offer or amendment if the original offer at the closing date is unsuccessful unless invited to do so by the seller's solicitor. However a purchaser's solicitor would not be acting improperly in submitting an offer prior to a closing date[3] and the seller's solicitor would not be acting improperly in acting on instructions to accept such an offer even though a closing date may have been fixed.

These guidelines were issued in 1991 in a buoyant housing market: perhaps a more common problem now is a purchaser instructing the solicitor to delay or withdraw from conclusion of missives. The solicitor is bound to act in accordance with the instructions of the client and could not therefore, either as a matter of law or professional practice, conclude missives on

---

1. Professional Practice Committee 1.11.93.
2. Professional Practice Committee 7.7.94.
3. Professional Practice Committee 5.5.94.

behalf of the principal. However in this as in all cases, if the solicitor feels that professional standards, including the maintenance of professional relations with a colleague, have been unduly compromised by acting in accordance with the client's instructions, the solicitor should consider whether to then withdraw from acting for the client altogether.

The delay in concluding missives frequently arises because the parties are negotiating on a number of extraneous matters of varying importance. In an effort to reduce delays the Law Society in 1992 issued a style offer and standard conditions for residential property, but these have never gained widespread acceptance. Nevertheless the revised guidelines which precede these are a useful statement of good practice. Where commercial property transactions are concerned, each is so individual that a standard form would be inappropriate.

While the domestic conveyancer might deplore the introduction of clauses dealing with carpets and cookers, for the commercial client matters such as rights of access and parking and the status and condition of fittings and fixtures are far more significant and it is realistic to expect that negotiation may be protracted and detailed. It is neither unusual nor bad practice for missives to be concluded only as the transaction settles if matters are genuinely still at issue, but to hold off conclusion of missives simply because the client perceives this as delivering a commercial advantage is sailing close to the wind.

Cheques and other documents

ACCOUNT

It is difficult to be dogmatic about whether or not the solicitor is entitled to stop a cheque on a client's account and each case depends on its merits but in general a solicitor should only stop such a cheque in exceptional circumstances. Cheques can only be drawn on the client account if there are client funds available: the only circumstances in which a cheque could be stopped because of shortage of funds is therefore where the cheque was drawn on the firm or the solicitor's personal account. In 1994 the Tribunal made a finding of professional misconduct where a solicitor drew cheques on his personal account where he ought to have known they would be dishonoured[1].

It should be noted that it is a standard condition of some lenders that the solicitor must be in funds to meet the purchase price and all costs, including stamp duty, before encashing the loan cheque. Even where that is not the case, the solicitor should not encash the loan cheque unless in a position to record a valid disposition and security. Accordingly, even where the solicitor's firm is not in funds, it has a duty to the lender for whom it acts to pay the stamp duty and meet recording dues for recording a disposition or security as soon as reasonably practicable.

The practice of sending cheques and documents as undelivered 'avoids alternative courses of action such as bridging for one day, instructing local agents or effecting settlement in person, all of which can be viewed as adding expense'. Against this background the Council, after considerable debate, has come to the view that where a cheque or document has been sent as undelivered, it is professional misconduct to encash the cheque or use the document in breach of that condition. This is so even where the condition is unilaterally imposed by the sender and is not therefore a term of the original contract, although it is also considered to be improper professional practice on the part of the sender to impose such a unilateral condition in the absence of prior agreement[2].

LETTERS OF OBLIGATION

Like the practice of sending documents as undelivered, the delivery of letters of obligation from one solicitor to another is recognised as an essential tool for the progress of transactions, chiefly, although not exclusively, in conveyancing transactions. Letters of obligation are in effect a guarantee by one solicitor to another, and should not be given unless the obligation undertaken is one with which the solicitor can personally comply or can control.

1. 1994 Annual Report of the Discipline Tribunal, p 5.
2. Professional Practice 1994 JLSS 470.

A 'classic' letter of obligation is one:

'in which the seller's solicitor undertakes to provide to the purchaser's solicitor a clear search brought down to a period of 14 days after the date of settlement, the delivery of a duly recorded discharge of the seller's standard security/securities and (if appropriate) a Feu Duty Redemption certificate.[1]'

Because of their practical importance, claims arising from 'classic' letters of obligation have been afforded cover under the Master Policy. This has been interpreted to mean not only letters of obligation delivered by the solicitor of the seller to the purchaser, but also the increasingly common situation where one solicitor acting for a co-owner transferring to another grants a letter of obligation to the solicitor acting for the other co-owner. A solicitor who grants a letter of obligation which does not constitute a 'classsic 'letter of obligation is obliged to pay a double deductible or excess in respect of any claim which is covered by the Master Policy and the claim itself forms part of the claims record, possibly leading to a loading on future premiums. A 'classic' letter of obligation attracts neither excess nor loading provided the solicitor has undertaken due inquiry, which includes a search in the computerised presentment book, before the granting of such a letter[2].

Failure to implement a letter of obligation can be professional misconduct. Where a solicitor failed to implement a letter because he had not retained sufficient funds to effect redemption of a feu duty, the Tribunal held that he should have used his own funds and was guilty of professional misconduct for persistent delay[3]. It should be noted that the Law Society has no power as such to require a solicitor to implement a letter of obligation – it can only deal with the matter as a disciplinary offence. Failure to implement a letter may therefore be professional misconduct but that does not necessarily achieve the result which the addressee of the letter requires.

1. Letter from the Secretary of the Law Society to all members of the profession, 30.1.1995.
2. Letter from the President of the Law Society, 30.1.1995.
3. 1992 Annual Report of the Discipline Tribunal, p 4.

Advertising

The restrictions on advertising have largely been removed and in terms of the 1991 Rules[1] solicitors can now promote their services in any way they think fit. However this is against a background that the Advertising Rules 'take into account the need to maintain mutual trust and confidence while permitting solicitors to market their services effectively and compete with each other'[2].

Accordingly, the rules do not permit solicitors to claim superiority for their services or practice over those offered by another solicitor, for example by using words such as 'best' and 'greatest'. An advertisement must not compare fees with those of another solicitor and must not contain any factual or misleading statements. A solicitor may state that he or she 'specialises in' a certain type of work, if this is justified by significantly greater knowledge and expertise than would be expected from a solicitor who does not so specialise. Only those accredited by the Law Society may use the specific designation 'Law Society Accredited Specialist in . . .'. The advertisement may not identify any client or business without the client's prior written consent, nor must either the material or the method of advertising be such as to bring the profession into disrepute. The advertisement must not be defamatory or illegal.

Any advertisement or promotional material issued by solicitors is deemed to have been issued with their approval, and it is therefore extremely unwise for a solicitor to delegate any final decision to an advertising agency even if the contract specifies that the agency shall have due regard to the Advertising Rules.

Many of the problems which still arise in relation to advertising concern distribution of promotional material rather than content. Earlier rules had expressly forbidden 'touting': although this phrase is no longer used, rule 5 still prohibits a direct or indirect approach to a person or persons 'whom a solicitor knows or ought reasonably to know, to be the client of another solicitor'. This does not preclude the general

---

1. Solicitors (Scotland)(Advertising and Promotion) Practice Rules 1991.
2. Code of Conduct, r 9.

circulation of promotional material by a solicitor, although many advertisers would now say that a general mailshot was an ineffective form of advertising and that 'targeted mailshots' were to be preferred. It is debatable at what point a targeted mailshot, for example to companies belonging to a particular trade association, falls foul of rule 5 but generally if the mailshot was distributed to all members it would be regarded as general circulation. It is arguable that any successful company must have its own solicitor, but conversely it is unrealistic to expect that all clients will necessarily remain with their original solicitors and the point of advertising at all is to open up competition between solicitors as well as between solicitors and estate agents, independent financial advisers, accountants etc.

A particular problem arises where solicitors wish to advertise their services outwith Scotland. Within the European Union the UK profession has the most liberal advertising regime and it may well be that an advertisement acceptable in the UK would be deemed unacceptable in another member state. This can cause problems for lawyers with foreign offices or in European groupings, which are now relatively common. A solicitor with an office in a host state is required to abide by the rules of that host state, and it has been held that each member state is entitled

'to determine how the balance should be struck between protection of the requirements of the proper administration of justice, the dignity of the legal profession, the right of everyone to receive information about legal services and affording lawyers the possibility of advertising their practices.'

Nevertheless UK lawyers have argued that restrictions on advertising are a bar to competition within the EC and may derive support from the Commission decision that the liberal professions are not exempt from competition rules, which may include restrictions on advertising as well as price agreements[2]. On the other hand, Scottish lawyers have argued that the ban by solicitors property centres on joint advertising by solicitors and estate agents is not restrictive of competition since the property centres are not themselves offering any legal services but are merely a medium for advertising.

1. *Casado Coca v Spain* [1994] 18 EHRR 1.
2. C/046/M/B/COPI.

In addition to the Advertising Rules, the Code of Conduct[1] makes it clear that it is improper to write directly to another solicitor's client, whether or not for the purpose of obtaining a mandate.

Other parties

As noted earlier[2], there is not ordinarily any duty of care to the opponent in the context of contentious proceedings, although exceptionally a duty might be created if the solicitor stepped outside that role to act, say, as custodian[3]. Where funds are deposited in joint names to await a contingency, for example completion of common repairs, the solicitor, in the absence of any specific contractual provisions, has a duty to obtain a reasonable rate of interest on funds deposited[4].

A solicitor is entitled to exercise a lien against the client and all third parties. It is not improper for a solicitor to exercise a lien over documents belonging to a client who is sequestrated provided that the solicitor is not also acting for the heritable creditor. As noted earlier, the solicitor cannot maintain that claim against third parties who are entitled to production as against the client, for example an office holder of the company in terms of the Insolvency Act 1986, ss 234–237.

It has traditionally been said – and reaffirmed at the Law Society's AGM in 1993 - that the solicitor has a professional duty to meet the fees of other professional persons, including surveyors and sheriff officers, for work instructed on behalf of clients, despite the fact that the rules of agency suggest that an agent is not liable for the debts of a disclosed principal[5]. There is more logic in the rule that solicitors are responsible for the fees of counsel, since counsel have traditionally not been able to sue in respect of their own fees. However if the solicitor makes it clear that he or she is acting only as agent and the

---

1. Rule 9.
2. See p 83.
3. *Al Kandari v JR Brown & Co* [1988] 1 All ER 833.
4. Professional Practice Committee 4.6.92.
5. 1983 JLSS 466.

third party accepts instructions on that basis, the solicitor should not be held liable.

Traditionally the solicitor has had an obligation to meet recording dues. However from 1995 the Registers of Scotland introduces a requirement for recording dues to be prepaid, in which case it may be more difficult to argue that there is a professional duty on the solicitor to discharge the recording dues in the absence of payment by the client, at least where the solicitor acts only for the purchaser and not for the lender as well. It is a condition of some lenders that the solicitor be in possession of recording dues before encashing the loan cheque, in which case it would undoubtedly be and continue to be a breach of contract to proceed without being in funds to meet those dues. It is open to debate whether the solicitor owes a similar duty in respect of fees due to the Companies Office, for example for filing an annual return, and it is certainly prudent for the solicitor to obtain funds in advance in any case where outlays are required whether or not there is a professional duty to meet these.

10. Fee charging

Fee charging

The necessary corollary of the obligation to provide an adequate professional service should be that the solicitor is entitled to an adequate professional fee, and to be fairly remunerated for the work undertaken.

The Law Society's Table of Fees for Conveyancing and General Business now recommends a scale fee only for summary complaints under the Road Traffic Acts and for extra-judicial settlements. In other cases it recommends that the solicitor may charge the account in detailed charges expressed in units or 'according to circumstances'. The Law Society recommends the value of a unit (in effect recommending an hourly charge) but even here, some items are expressed to be 'according to circumstances'. In any case, the rule is that the fees charged by solicitors must be fair and reasonable in all the circumstances of a transaction, and this same principle applies whether this be the conduct of litigation, a company takeover or a domestic conveyance. In determining what is fair and reasonable the sum to be charged should take into consideration

(1) the importance of the matter to the client;
(2) the amount or value of any money or property involved;
(3) the complexity of the matter or the difficulty or novelty of the questions raised;
(4) the skill, labour, specialised knowledge and responsibility involved on the part of the solicitor or assistant;
(5) the time expended;
(6) the length, number and importance of any documents or other papers prepared or perused; and
(7) the place where and the circumstances in which the services or any part thereof are rendered, including the degree of expedition required.

Further guidance is given in general regulation 5 and in the Appendix to the Table of Fees (reproduced as Appendix 2). However what is regarded by the solicitor as fair and reasonable is not the determining factor: if there is a dispute as to the amount of a fee it is competent for the client to refer the matter to taxation by the auditor of court. The solicitor may choose to refer the matter to the auditor, and must do so before a decree will be granted for recovery of fees whether in absence or *in foro*[1]. The auditor should take into account the same factors, although in coming to a view it is of course open to the auditor to reduce or increase the fee proposed[2].

As between party and party, the normal rule is that the unsuccessful party is found liable to pay the other party's costs, but subject to the constraints of the Table of Fees. The successful solicitor may apply to the court for authority for payment of an additional fee, that is in addition to the amount charged in accordance with the Table of Fees. If authority is granted, the auditor in the Court of Session is directed to take into account identical factors in determining the additional fee but with the additional criteria of 'the steps taken with a view to settling the litigation, limiting the matters in dispute or limiting the scope of the hearing'[3]. In the sheriff court, the sheriff may direct an increase in the fee authorised by the Table of Fees[4] and is also directed to take into account the same factors with the additional criteria that there shall also be considered 'any other fees and allowances payable to the solicitor in respect of other items in the same litigation and otherwise charged in the account'.

Where the unsuccessful party is legally aided, the liability for costs may be reduced to nil on the motion of his or her counsel or agent[5]. In that case, the solicitor acting for the successful party may make application for costs to be met by SLAB. The possible protection against an award of costs is one of the most important reasons for a solicitor advising a client at the outset of a case whether legal aid is available.

---

1. *Lyall and Wood v Thomson* 1993 SLT (Sh Ct) 21; but see R Mays ' A taxing time for solicitors' 1993 SLT 249.
2. But see 'Written fee-charging agreements', p 110.
3. Act of Sederunt 1965, SI 1965/321, as amended July 1993.
4. Act of Sederunt 1989, SI 1989/434, as amended July 1993.
5. Legal Aid (Scotland) Act 1986, s 18(2).

Estimates

Where a client is given a verbal estimate of the fee for a transaction, it is strongly recommended that this be confirmed in writing as soon as possible. This not only keeps the client properly informed at the outset, but reduces the scope for disagreement at a later date. The estimate should also make it clear what outlays the client should expect to meet and when. It should also be made clear to the client whether the initial interview forms a part of the services rendered: if the matter does not proceed further, the client may be entitled to view the initial interview as simply an unsuccessful attempt by the solicitor to sell the solicitor's services. However where the solicitor has rendered valuable advice (which may quite responsibly be not to proceed with a claim or a defence) the solicitor should be entitled to charge.

Although this is entirely a matter for the solicitor, it seems prudent to set a financial ceiling for work in progress and/or outlays and to render interim accounts throughout the conduct of a long running transaction. The solicitor is otherwise acting as the client's banker, with adverse effects for the solicitor's cash flow in the short to medium term and the uncomfortable prospect in the longer term of being an unsecured creditor should the client for some reason fail to pay the final account when rendered. Many clients also prefer interim billing as it assists their own cash flow. Interim billing has the additional benefit of acting as a cross check on any file review system, reducing the possibility of overlooking a file and possibly missing a critical time limit.

The solicitor should make it clear that, particularly where litigation is involved, no estimate can be accurate because so much depends upon the opposing party. Much also depends upon the client: if the client telephones the solicitor every day, that time will be reflected in the final account, and it is here that accurate records are particularly important. It should also be made clear whether posts and incidents are to be charged in addition to any hourly rate. Although the Table of Fees permits the charging of posts and incidents in addition to the hourly rate, this is viewed by many clients as an anomaly in the context of a solicitor-client account. It can convincingly be argued that the cost of telephone, faxes etc is simply an overhead which should be taken into account in calculating the hourly rate or fee to be charged, and it is only appropriate to add this where there was an extraordinary item, for example courier charges.

Estimates should also make clear whether or not the fee quoted is inclusive or exclusive of VAT. Although it is reasonable to assume that commercial clients are registered for VAT, and are able to recover any VAT paid on the solicitor's account, private clients are unlikely to be registered and will rightly resent what they see as the imposition of an additional fee. The usual rule applies and if there is no course of dealing or legitimate assumption, and the position is not made clear, a quotation of fee is deemed inclusive of VAT.

Where the client is legally aided, the solicitor should make it clear that SLAB has a first charge on sums recovered or preserved. When acting for a pursuer (whether legally aided or not) the solicitor should also make it clear that sums recovered may have to be repaid to the Compensation Recovery Unit.

Recovery of solicitor's fees

The solicitor who is in funds may not transfer funds from the client account until a fee note has been issued, although transfer does not preclude the client subsequently challenging the account[1]. A solicitor has a duty to supervise the issue of fee notes by any member of staff and has a particular duty to supervise the issue of fee notes when acting under a power of attorney[2].

The solicitor acting as trustee must have authority in terms of the trust deed to charge separately for services as solicitor, and this applies whether the trust is a testamentary trust or not. Particular attention should be given to the terms of any charitable trust or the memorandum and articles of a charitable company limited by guarantee: if the position is not clear, there is the risk that charitable status may be jeopardised if the solicitor is remunerated by the charity.

---

1. Solicitors (Scotland) Accounts Rules 1995, r 6 (1)(d).
2. *MacColl v Council of the Law Society of Scotland* 1987 SLT 525.

Where the client has not paid the fee then, as indicated above, it is not normally competent for the solicitor to obtain a decree without first remitting the account to taxation. The cost of the auditor's fee is recovered by the solicitor if the account is taxed at the same or more as the account rendered, which can mean that it is not cost effective for the client to challenge a taxation. However where there is a written fee-charging agreement in place, it is not competent for the court to remit the account for taxation, although a written fee-charging agreement may not include a warrant for execution.

Where the solicitor is apprehensive that recovery from the client may be difficult, for example because the client is based in a different jurisdiction, the solicitor for the successful party in an action is entitled to seek an award of expenses against the opponent in the solicitor's own name as agent-disburser on the basis that there is an implied assignation of the right to expenses by the client to the agent[1]. The solicitor can also request the court to hold the solicitor entitled to a charge upon and payment out of any property which has been recovered or preserved by the solicitor in the action or proceeding, and the court may make such order for the taxation of and for the payment of expenses out of the property as the court thinks fit[2]. Where the court has made such a declaration, any attempt by the client to circumvent the order, for example by a voluntary transfer or grant of a deed, is void as against the charge or right, except where in favour of a bona fide purchaser or lender[3].

Debt factoring is not permitted either by buying a client's debts – in which case there is a clear conflict of interest – or by selling the solicitor's debts – which would involve a breach of confidentiality and breach of the Practice Rules prohibiting sharing of fees[4].

Sanctions

Where the solicitor has issued an account for professional fees and outlays which is grossly excessive (whether or not the

1. MacLaren *Court of Session Practice* (1916) p 27.
2. Solicitors (Scotland) Act 1980, s 62(1).
3. Ibid, s 62(2).
4. Professional Practice Committee 8.1.93.

account has been paid by or on behalf of the client or debited by the solicitor) the Council has the power to withdraw the solicitor's practising certificate, so that the solicitor is suspended from practice[1]. That suspension is terminated where the Council is satisfied that the solicitor has submitted the account for taxation and refunded any excess amount, but even so the Council is not required to terminate the suspension where it is of the opinion that the solicitor is liable to disciplinary proceedings. The Council is entitled to be represented at the diet of taxation and to make representations to the Auditor of Court and costs may be deemed to follow success. Where the amount due as taxed is the amount specified in the original account, the Council is required to pay the Auditor's fee but 'in any other case'(which would seem to include the unlikely scenario where the fee was increased) the solicitor concerned is to pay the Auditor's fee[2].

The Council also has the power under the Legal Aid (Scotland) Act 1986, s 31(3) to prohibit a solicitor from acting in legal aid matters and this has been used against solicitors who have demonstrated an abuse of the legal aid scheme.

Where the Council upholds a complaint that the solicitor has provided an inadequate professional service, the Council has the power to reduce the amount of fees and outlays recoverable by the solicitor to nil or such amount as the Council may specify, in addition to requiring the solicitor to take certain action including the payment of up to £1,000 compensation[3]. The intention was that this would cover claims which did not necessarily amount to negligence (although they might do so) but would benefit from a speedy out of court resolution. In most respects the system appears to work well, although the very considerable time which is taken up with any complaint can be excessive in relation to minor claims. While accepting that any complainer may have a legitimate grievance, from the point of view of the Council, it is perhaps unfortunate that there is no *de minimis* provision.

Far from charging fees which are too high, the perception amongst the profession is that many solicitors are charging

1. Solicitors (Scotland) Act 1980, s 39A.
2. Ibid, s 39A (6).
3. Ibid, s 42A.

fees which are too low. Many solicitors now refuse to under-take legal aid work, because the rates are so low and the regu-lations so complex. In the field of domestic conveyancing, the problem is one of too many solicitors and a stagnant housing market which has led to cut-throat competition and undercut-ting of fees. It is hard to think that even the most efficient prac-tice can process the work involved in properly investigating the title and all the ancillary matters for the fees sometimes charged. The issue was debated at length at the Law Society's 1995 AGM where it was argued not only that some referral schemes depressed fees to an extent that the quality of service offered to the client was affected (and an undue burden was placed on the other solicitors involved in such transactions), but also that over-reliance on third party introductions com-promised the independence of solicitors participating in these referral schemes. The proponents of this view feel the problem is exacerbated by the very large advertising budgets of the third party introducers such as estate agents, which effectively subsidise the solicitors who participate in referral schemes and thus distort competition between solicitors. The counter-argu-ment is that efficient office systems and investment in technol-ogy has been such that some solicitors can process business profitably even at these low levels of fee and the ability to do so is simply an example of efficient practice management and of true competition in operation. There is as yet no statistical evidence that cut-price fees have led to an increase in negli-gence claims or even an increase in complaints from clients.

Written fee-charging agreements

The 1980 Act, s 61A(1)[1] provides that:

'where a solicitor and his client have reached an agreement in writing as to the solicitor's fees in respect of any work done or to be done by him for his client, it shall not be competent, in any litigation arising out of any dispute as to the amount due to be paid under any such agreement, for the court to remit the solicitor's account for taxation.'

1. Inserted by the Law Reform (Miscellaneous Provisions) (Scotland) Act 1990, s 39(3).

The Solicitors (Scotland) (Written Fee-Charging Agreements) Practice Rules 1993 make it clear that the form of the agreement is a matter for the solicitor and client, save that a written fee-charging agreement may not contain a clause consenting to warrant for preservation and execution. It was felt at the time of passing the Rules that to permit such a clause gave the solicitor too considerable an advantage and that the solicitor should still require to obtain a decree before proceeding to diligence, even though it is not competent for the court to remit the account for taxation. It is still competent for the client to challenge that the work in question had in fact been done and that the time claimed (if charged at an hourly / daily rate) had in fact been spent, and these issues would be a matter for proof.

An agreement may stipulate a fixed charge in respect of any particular work. However in many cases it is not appropriate to charge on this basis and both solicitor and client prefer that work is charged on an hourly basis. To constitute a valid agreement under the 1980 Act, s 61A, the hourly or daily rate should be specifically related to legal work done or to be done and not simply quoted in the abstract[1].The agreement itself can be constituted either by exchange of letters or by a written acceptance of the client[2] although it does not have to be probative.

Speculative actions

It is well established in Scotland that both solicitors and advocates may act on a speculative basis, whereby no fee is payable unless the action is successful. This should be distinguished from contingency-fee agreements whereby the fee is directly related to and recoverable out of any sums awarded or agreed. The contingency-fee system is common in the USA (where there is no comparable rule that the unsuccessful party is liable

1. See R C Mckenzie 'Written fee-charging agreements' 1994 SLT 213 which includes style agreements.
2. For the comparable English position see *Chamberlain v Boodle & King (a firm)* [1982] 3 All ER 188.

for the successful party's costs) but in Scotland contingency-fee agreements are deemed contrary to law and void on the grounds of public policy. Speculative actions on the other hand are encouraged on the basis that they make available advice and assistance that would not otherwise be available, although it may occasionally be difficult to see the distinction.

The solicitor who has acted for a party on a speculative basis is entitled to seek an additional fee to reflect the assumption of risk. The solicitor and client may agree that in the event that a litigation undertaken on a speculative basis is successful, the solicitor's fee shall be increased by a percentage which may not exceed the limits prescribed by Act of Sederunt. In terms of the relevant Acts of Sederunt[1] the increase may be up to 100 per cent of fees on a party and party basis and although there may be nothing in the Acts to stop a solicitor charging 100 per cent for each and every action, this may not reflect the appropriate fee in all the circumstances. In some cases it may appear to be excessive: in others it may be too little since the basis is party and party expenses, not an agent and client basis. This therefore excludes fees for work before the litigation commenced – copying fees, the cost of non-essential meetings and telephone calls with clients – all of which may be considerable. An alternative to this somewhat unattractive option is for the solicitor to elect to charge on an agent and client basis and to argue before the Auditor for a fee which is 'fair and reasonable in all the circumstances of the case' or to enter into a written fee-charging agreement with the client which sets out an acceptable basis for enhanced remuneration taking into account the assumption of risk by the solicitor (but which is still not grossly excessive in terms of the Solicitors (Scotland) Act 1980, s 39A[2]).

Other factors which make the speculative action less attractive than might appear at first sight include the obligation of solicitors to meet the fees of counsel (although counsel may agree to act on a similar basis) and outlays such as court dues (where that option is not available). The obligation to meet the opponent's expenses should the action fail means that a client who qualifies for legal aid (and is therefore protected against

---

1. SI 1992/1879 for the sheriff court and SI 1992/1898 for the Court of Session.
2. See discussion in W G Semple 'Fees in speculative actions' 1994 JLSS 57.

an award of expenses) is unwise to proceed on a speculative basis. It may shortly be possible to obtain insurance against being found liable for an opponent's costs but the experience of insurers in the UK legal expenses insurance market has not been particularly happy. There are also unacceptable public policy implications if private insurance is seen as an alternative to a properly funded legal aid scheme.

There may occasionally be confusion in as much as the phrase 'contingent fee basis' may also be used to include a speculative fee basis: that appears to be the meaning of the UK accountants' institutes in issuing guidance to their members that it would not be appropriate for an accountant acting as an expert witness to charge 'on a contingent fee basis'[1]. Equally it does not seem appropriate for solicitors to act on a speculative basis in any case where they are giving a professional opinion as a witness, since they have a material interest in the outcome which might be seen (whether or not this was the fact) to influence their evidence.

Scale fees and other pricing mechanisms

As observed above, scale fees have been abolished except in a few restricted areas. For those that remain it may be noted that the European Commission has held that a mandatory tariff for services provided by customs agents (who classify themselves as a profession) constituted an infringement of article 85(1)[2] although this is currently[3] being appealed.

Although hourly rates or scale fees are the most usual way of pricing legal services, other acceptable methods of pricing may be agreed. These include general or specific retainers, discounts for bulk transactions, fixed fees and averaged rates at which all fee earners are charged regardless of seniority. It is for the solicitor and client to negotiate the pricing mechanism for the transaction, within the limits of acceptable public policy.

1. CAJEC Consultation Paper 'Corporate finance: due diligence and contingent fees' (1994).
2. Consiglio natzionale degli spedizionieri dognalio (CSND) OJ 13.8.93 L203/27.
3. February 1995.

For investment business the solicitor is required to disclose to the client the method by which the solicitor is to be remunerated, including any commission payable[1]. As noted earlier, this is merely an example of the general rule that the solicitor, as agent, may not make a secret profit from the client.

1. See p 126.

11. Financial regulation and accounting

Accounts

Solicitors are required to account to their clients for all funds held by them and many of the Law Society rules are no more than detailed expressions of this general rule of agency. All solicitors in private practice are required to observe the Solicitors (Scotland) Accounts Rules 1995[1]. The Rules do not apply to solicitors in employment, as defined in the 1980 Act, s 35(1)(4) as regards monies received, held or paid by them in the course of their employment, but there will undoubtedly be internal accounting procedures which they are required to observe.

Every solicitor who holds clients' money is required to maintain a separate client account or accounts into which all client monies exceeding £50 require to be paid into without delay. The most important of the Accounts Rules is rule 4(1)(a) which requires the solicitor to ensure that at all times, the sum at credit of the client account(s) shall be not less than the total of the client's money held by the solicitor. The solicitor may maintain an overdraft in the client's name with the client's written authority, and where the solicitor does so that overdraft is not taken into account in calculating the overall client surplus. Client funds must be available for the client when required and if monies are to be deposited in name of the solicitor for the client, this should be on no more than one month's call unless the solicitor has express written authority to the contrary.

The purpose of the Rules is to ensure that the solicitor has sufficient funds in the client account to meet the aggregate of all the monies due by the solicitor to individual clients and that this can be demonstrated from an examination of the solicitor's books.

---

1. Made under the Solicitors (Scotland) Act 1980, ss 34-36.

'It is not simply a matter of maintaining solvency and it is not acceptable merely to demonstrate that funds are due and payable which will have the effect of producing funds...it is an essential feature of the Accounts Rules that it can be demonstrated from the books themselves that a solicitor has sufficient funds on the client account and this cannot be so if the solicitor requires to rely on funds which he has still to receive in order to achieve a credit balance.'[1]

The Rules set out what monies may legitimately be withdrawn from the client account, but subject to the overriding proviso that money belonging to one client is not withdrawn without written authority for the purpose of meeting a payment to or on behalf of another client[2]. Although withdrawals may include money required for or to account of a debt due by a solicitor to a client:

(1) A solicitor is not entitled to withdraw sums in respect of recording dues until receipt by the solicitor of the Keeper's invoice. As it may be some time before this invoice is received (although less now than some years ago) the effect of withdrawal before receipt of the Keeper's invoice is that the client was in effect making an interest free loan to the solicitor. Conversely a solicitor is entitled to require a client to provide monies to account to prevent the situation where the solicitor is otherwise providing the client with an interest free loan to meet stamp duty, recording dues, court fees etc[3].

(2) A solicitor is entitled to withdraw money 'properly required for or to account of the solicitor's professional account' if the fee has been debited to the ledger account in the solicitor's books and a copy of the account has been rendered[4]. Normally this means a fee note has been sent to the client, but note the possibility of taxation if the client does not agree with the account and there is not a fee-charging agreement in place. Moreover the court has made it clear that 'money can never be "properly required" for payment of a bogus account however neatly it has been debited to the client's ledger account. The pre-

1. Tribunal decision 770/89.
2. Solicitors (Scotland) Accounts Rules 1995, r 6(1)
3. Ibid, r 6(1)(b) and (2).
4. Ibid, r 6(1)(d).

supposition of the Rule properly construed is that the solicitor's account therein mentioned is a fair and reasonable one subject only perhaps to minor criticisms of detail'[1]. The charging of excessive fees may in itself lead to disciplinary proceedings, although the solicitor may not necessarily be in breach of the Accounts Rules and the fact that an account has been rendered and money debited does not prevent the Council finding under the 1980 Act, s 39A that professional fees and outlays charged have been grossly excessive and may require to be refunded to the client. A solicitor who is under a duty to supervise may not escape a finding of professional misconduct where excessive fees are charged by a subordinate, even though the solicitor did not personally know excessive fees were being charged[1].

(3) It is not acceptable practice for a solicitor to draw a cheque on the client account in anticipation of funds which may be received later that day or shortly thereafter. It is 'the essence of the Rules that a solicitor is only entitled to draw the money from his client account if he holds funds for that client or he has in his possession a cheque which he will deposit in his client account for behoof of his client later that same day'[2].

(4) Where money is drawn from the client account, both the ledger and the cheque itself must record the name or account number of the person whose account is to be credited[3].

Records

A solicitor is required at all times to keep properly written-up books and accounts to show all dealings with clients' money whether through the client account or other dealings. The books and accounts must show the movement of funds for each client separately and must be recorded not simply in a clients' cash book but also in a separate record of ledger transfers. Although certain sums may not require to be paid into the

1. *MacColl v Law Society of Scotland* 1987 SLT 525.
2. Tribunal decision 770/89.
3. Accounts Rules, r 6 (3)

client account, the solicitor has an obligation to record clients' money held or received, including cheques etc payable to a third party on behalf of a client which relates to a transaction involving heritable property that is an obligation[1].

In addition a solicitor is required to keep properly written up books and accounts to show the true financial position of the practice. There is no insolvency testing of solicitors personally, but the Council may apply for the appointment of a judicial factor if on investigation it is satisfied that in connection with a solicitor's practice as such, liabilities exceed assets and with this in mind the 1995 Accounts Rules introduced a requirement for each solicitor to balance his or her books monthly, not simply annually[2]. The Council is also entitled to apply for the appointment of a judicial factor if the 'books, accounts and other documents are in such a condition that it is not reasonably practicable to ascertain definitely whether his liabilities exceed his assets'[3].

Where monies are received or payments made under a power of attorney, a solicitor is required to maintain a register of powers of attorney and to submit a list of any powers of attorney granted during the accounting period together with the accountant's certificate[4].

A solicitor is required to reconcile client bank statements and client ledger and bank balances at intervals not exceeding one month and to retain reconciliation statements and lists of balances for a period of 18 months from the date they were carried out[5]. In addition, every 3 months a solicitor is required to reconcile cash books or ledger accounts with client passbooks, building society printouts, and any other special deposit or specified accounts. Again there is a requirement to retain those reconciliation statements for 18 months. The Tribunal has made it clear that it takes a serious view of a failure to institute and regularly monitor a system of making monthly reconciliations[6]. Reconciliation requirements apply to client balances,

1. Accounts Rules, r 7.
2. Ibid, r 12 (4)(b)
3. 1980 Act, s 41.
4. Accounts Rules, r 11.
5. Ibid, r 13.
6. Tribunal decision 858/93.

however small, and should not be overlooked simply because the balances are residual balances in an executry or old trust account or because the bank or building society where the funds are held does not provide automatic monthly statements.

Prohibitions

In addition to the general rules, certain classes of financial transactions attract specific regulation.

(1) A solicitor may not borrow money from a client unless the client is in the business of lending money or the client has been independently advised as to the making of the loan. The solicitor is otherwise open to an accusation of undue influence and gross conflict of interest.

(2) A solicitor may not act for the lender of a loan to be secured over heritable property advanced or to be advanced to the solicitor or any of a designated class, all closely connected with the solicitor[1]. This prohibition extends to an obligation *ad factum praestandum* or any obligation to pay money, and not only to the creation but also the variation, assignation or discharge of a relevant standard security[2].

Investigation

Every firm must appoint a designated cash room partner or partners responsible for compliance by the firm of the Accounts Rules[3].

Every firm to which the Accounts Rules apply is now required to balance their books monthly[4], as well as at least once a year, and deliver to the Council within six months of the

1. Accounts Rules, r 10(1).
2. Ibid, r 10 (2).
3. Ibid, r 18.
4. Ibid, r 12 (4)(b).

completion of that accounting period, an accountant's certificate in respect of that period. These time limits are therefore more stringent than those for private companies who have a period of ten months within which to produce audited accounts, although the Council has the power to grant an extension, not to exceed a further six months.

The accountants must investigate and satisfy themselves that the solicitor has complied with the relevant rules and it is not sufficient for the accountant to rely on the representations of the solicitor without conducting independent inquiry. Where an accountant fails to draw attention to the solicitor's failure to comply with the relevant rules, the Council may refuse to accept further accountant's certificates granted by such an accountant. The certificate is addressed to the practice, and aggrieved partners (or their insurers) who feel an accountant's inspection should have disclosed a fraud by one of the partners or staff might argue the duty of care was owed to the partners jointly and severally, subject of course to arguments as to their contributory negligence. Moreover it is clear that the Council relies on the accountant's representations: accordingly where there has been negligence by the accountant in failing to detect obvious failures to observe the rules there is a strong argument that the accountant may be liable to the Council and in particular the Guarantee Fund if the Fund makes an award in respect of fraud which should have been revealed by the accountant's inspection[1]. Whether the duty of care extends to individual clients of the practice, including claimants on the Guarantee Fund, is debatable but seems unlikely.

A solicitor who conducts investment business must also provide a separate compliance certificate from an independent accountant, certifying that the solicitor was not in breach of the Financial Services Act 1986; Solicitors (Conduct of Investment Business) Practice Rules 1994; and the Solicitors (Scotland) Investment Business Training Regulations 1994. Certified persons[2] must submit a management letter to the inspecting accountant in advance of the examination, which letter is used

---

1. *Capro Industries plc v Dickman* [1990] 1 All ER 568; *Morgan Crucible Co plc v Hill Samuel Bank Ltd* [1990] 3 All ER 330; *Galoo Ltd v Bright Grahame Murray* [1995] 1 All ER 16.
2. See p 122.

as the basis for the inspection. However the onus is again on the inspecting accountants to satisfy themselves that the certified person has complied with the rules.

The Council maintains its own team of inspectors and aims to inspect the books and accounts of each solicitor's practice at least once every two years. Where the inspection team is not satisfied with the results the solicitor may be asked to attend an interview or to resolve outstanding matters by correspondence, and the Council may require the solicitor to undergo a supplementary examination at the solicitor's own expense. Where the Council has conducted an inspection there is no requirement for the firm to produce an independent accountant's certificate or compliance certificate for the period.

The Council has the power to require production and delivery of all documents within the solicitor's control and demand explanations of the solicitor if satisfied that it is necessary to do so for the purpose of investigating a complaint. This may include a failure to comply with any of the Accounts Rules as well as other complaints as to professional misconduct, inadequate professional service etc[1].

As part of its risk management strategy for insurance purposes, in 1993 the Council undertook a comprehensive inspection of claims records under the Master Policy and firms were invited to respond on an individual basis. This has been followed up by establishment of a practice advisory team of experienced solicitors, with a remit to undertake further investigation in order to promote sound practice management throughout the profession.

---

1. 1980 Act, s 42C, inserted by the Solicitors (Scotland) Act 1988, s 2.

12. Investment business

Authorisation

Solicitors in the course of conducting investment business must observe (a) the Solicitors (Scotland) Investment Training Regulations 1994; (b) the Solicitors (Scotland) (Conduct of Investment Business) Practice Rules 1994; and (c) the Solicitors (Scotland) Compliance Certificate Rules 1994. The Conduct of Investment Business Rules in particular contain detailed practice notes which may be regarded as authoritative guidance as to how the Council considers the rule or paragraph would operate in particular circumstances, although the practice notes are not themselves part of the rule. It should be borne in mind that the Rules must comply with the requirements of the Securities and Investment Board, which grants recognition to the Society as a regulatory body.

From 1 November 1995 the Society will only authorise a firm to conduct investment business by issuing an Investment Business Certificate if there is a partner who is exempt from or has passed the Society's exam or holds an investment qualification equivalent to the Society's exam. The Investment Advice Certificate of the Securities Institute or the Financial Planning Certificate of the Chartered Insurance Institute will be recognised as an investment qualification for this purpose. All other solicitors and non-solicitors conducting investment business within an authorised firm must be qualified through exemption or the passing of a relevant examination.

In addition every solicitor or non-solicitor who is authorised to conduct investment business from 1 November 1995 is required to undertake five hours of continuing professional development in investment business per annum. This applies whether or not the holder has been exempted from undertaking an examination before issue of the Investment Business Certificate. The training can be in the form of private or group study and a separate record should be kept of compliance with this requirement.

Activities

Activities constituting investment business are defined in the Financial Services Act 1988[1] as:

(1) Dealing in investments, including buying/selling investments, either as principal or agent. There are limited exclusions including own account dealings and financial packages associated with the supply of goods and services. Also excluded is the sale of 75 per cent or more of private companies.
(2) Arranging deals in investments, for example introducing. Again there are limited exclusions, including an exclusion for trustees and executors unless separately remunerated for investment services.
(3) Managing investments. Exclusions include managing of investments by a trustee or executor unless he or she holds him or herself out as offering management investment services or is separately remunerated for providing these services.
(4) Advising on investments, that is giving persons in their capacity as investors or potential investors advice on the merits of their buying or selling of an investment. A particularly important exclusion includes the giving of advice in the course of a profession, giving of which is a necessary part of other advice or services given in the course of carrying on that profession (although this does not apply if the advice is separately remunerated).
(5) Establishing or winding up a collective investment scheme.

'Investments' as defined by the Financial Services Act 1988[2] includes company shares, debentures and certificates of deposit (but not building society shares or current, deposit or savings accounts with building societies) and naturally includes investments such as unit trusts, options and futures. It also includes long-term insurance contracts such as life insurance which are likely to be an integral part of house purchase transactions or the setting up of new partnerships or

1. Sch 1, Parts II, III.
2. Sch 1, Part I.

companies. Most solicitors are therefore likely to find that their activities will from time to time fall within the definition of conducting investment business unless they can take advantage of the exclusions, of which the most obvious is that the advice was an integral part of other professional advice. It is a matter of interpretation whether it is 'necessary' in the course of advising shareholders and partners in the course of setting up a new business, to advise on matters such as life insurance. Such advice is not necessary in the sense that it is not a legal requirement: on the other hand, most solicitors would take the view that such matters should be discussed with the client in the context of providing adequate professional services. The reference to 'other advice or services'indicates that such advice may be ancillary and it is hard to resist the argument that advice in such a context does not in itself constitute investment business. If the solicitor is asked to conduct investment business for which he or she is not authorised, the client must be passed to another independent adviser authorised by the Securities and Investment Board (SIB), whether another solicitor or an independent financial adviser. The exclusion is not available if the advice is separately remunerated, for example by commission.

A firm which holds an investment business certificate may do all manner of investment business with the exception of those activities specified in the Conduct of Investment Business Rules, rule 3.2. These are activities which fall well outside the normal scope of solicitors activities as such; for example acting as manager or trustee of a regulated collective investment scheme. A solicitor who wishes to act as manager or trustee requires authorisation by a regulatory body other than the Law Society. As from 1 July 1995, any certified person who wishes to give advice or make arrangements for a client in relation to a transfer or opt-out from an occupational pension scheme requires to obtain specific authorisation from the Society. This ring fencing of pension business applies to all individuals and firms authorised under the Financial Services Act 1986.

A firm may derive up to 49.9 per cent of its gross income from investment business and a record must be kept of this income[1]. Both fee income from clients and commission income

---

1. Conduct of Investment Business Rules, r 6.5.

from third parties such as brokers must be included in the calculation, even if the full benefit of the commission is passed to the client. In some cases, such as the sale and purchase of securities or an endowment policy, the investment business income is easy to calculate as being the share of commission together with any fee charged for the advice given. In other cases, for example in relation to an executry, a continuing trust or corporate client work, the calculation is more difficult.

Conduct of business

The Accounts Rules require that, subject to certain exceptions for corporate finance activities, for execution-only clients and for life assurance or unit-trust only clients, certified persons require to enter into a 'client terms of business' with any client to whom investment management services are provided. The terms of business must be in the form of a written contract where discretionary investment management is undertaken. This effectively deals with the application of client funds: the solicitor also has to comply with the requirements of the Money Laundering Regulations as regards both the source and the application of client funds[1]. The Conduct of Investment Business Rules, rule 4.4 imposes an obligation that, except when acting for an execution-only client, a certified person must take all reasonable steps to ensure that any investment recommendation or exercise of discretion on behalf of a client is suitable, having regard to the facts disclosed by the client and other relevant facts about the client of which the certified person is or should reasonably be aware. Thus the requirements to 'know the client' may overlap and inquiries which the solicitor should make in terms of the Money Laundering Regulations may be deemed facts of which the solicitor should have been aware under the Conduct of Investment Business Rules.

In addition rule 4.4 requires the certified person to take all reasonable steps to ensure that the client understands the nature of the risks involved in any investment transaction or the exercise of a discretionary power and, where the acquisi-

1. See p 135.

tion is a packaged product, the certified person must show there is no other investment which would be likely to secure the client's investment objectives more advantageously and that the client has information which is adequate to enable him or her to make an informed investment decision. The solicitor cannot be expected to ensure or require the client to follow this best advice, but if the client instructs otherwise, this should be made more than unusually clear in the client records. In any event, a solicitor is required to provide the client with key information about a packaged product at the time the recommendation is made[1] whether the product is issued by a UK or non-UK insurance company. This key information must be client specific, that is it has to relate to both the policy and the individual policy holder and if the life insurance company cannot produce this information, the solicitor is required to do so. The solicitor must also give the client an explanation in writing as to why the firm recommends that a client should take on or relinquish a long-term commitment[2]. This rule, which the Securities and Investment Board required all regulators to introduce, was imposed to stamp out the practice, believed to be widespread at the time of the 1980s property boom, of unscrupulous salesmen encouraging 'churning' or the unnecessary surrender of existing policies and the taking out of new policies for which the salesman received commission.

In addition, from 1 January 1995 the certified person is required to disclose in cash terms and in writing to the client the commission payable in respect of all life products whenever a recommendation is made. These 'hard disclosure' requirements apply to all sales agents, whatever their regulatory body. Moreover, the Rules prevent any solicitor from becoming tied exclusively to a particular life office, unit trust operator etc or giving or receiving gifts or services or any other benefits or inducements which might reasonably be regarded as likely to influence improperly the recommendation. This does not prohibit for instance commission-sharing arrangements with brokers but the commission should be returned to

---

1. Formerly product disclosure was required only before or as soon as reasonably practicable after the client bought the product.
2. Conduct of Investment Business Rules, r 4.4(3) as amended.

the client or reinvested, or if it is used indirectly to restrict the firm's fee, this should be notified to the client (and of course must be advised if relating to life insurance in any case). The Rules also require a certified person on or before recommending the investment services of any person to make full disclosure to the client of any material association, arrangement or relationship existing between the certified person and the person whose services are recommended. The solicitor must also disclose any material interest and obtain the client's consent before effecting a transaction in respect of which the solicitor has a material interest. All of this is effectively no more than a detailed expression of the general law of agency which prohibits the agent from making a secret profit and requires the benefit of any profit to be passed on to the client. If the solicitor does not make full disclosure, the principal is entitled at common law to require the solicitor as agent to account for such profits (not to mention the fact that the solicitor would undoubtedly be exposed to disciplinary proceedings).

Record keeping

A firm must keep copies of all investment advertisements issued or approved by it for at least five years[1]. For all investment transactions rule 6 imposes even stricter record keeping requirements. A firm is required to keep records for ten years of:

(1) all instructions received from clients to effect investment transactions and all decisions to effect transactions taken on behalf of clients;

(2) all instructions given to other persons to effect investment transactions on behalf of clients; and

(3) all investment transactions which have been effected on behalf of clients (for Stock Exchange transactions, this means keeping a copy of the relevant contract note).

Where a stockbroker is instructed to carry out a transaction on behalf of a client, the contract note should state that the

---

1. Conduct of Investment Business Rules, r 5.1(7).

transaction is to be so effected on behalf of a client[1]. Under Financial Services Act rules, the client as the identified principal is an indirect customer of the FSA authorised firm unless there is an agreement in writing between the FSA authorised firm and the agent to the contrary. In all other respects the solicitor-agent(and not his principal) is the customer of the FSA authorised firm. The solicitor-agent should retain a copy of all agreements with stockbrokers which should clearly state upon whom the obligations of best advice and best execution fall.

For life policies and unit trusts, the solicitor should record within the client's file that the essential details relating to the life policy or unit trust have been given to the client, either by the firm itself or the life or unit trust company. Under rule 6.6 the solicitor is required to maintain a separate record of the number of life policies and transactions in regulated collective investment schemes placed directly or indirectly with each individual life office and operator.

A separate record should be kept of all client documents of title relating to certificated and uncertificated securities, and a firm must be able to identify where any documents are kept as well as who is the beneficial owner of each of those investments to which the document relates. If the solicitor employs a third party to act as custodian of the client documents of title, that other person must provide a written undertaking of its compliance with rule 6.4 and this undertaking should be retained for ten years.

To ensure compliance with the rules, a certified person is required to establish and maintain rules and procedures (compliance procedures) by reference to which each officer and employee of the certified person can ensure that they comply with the rules and must review those procedures at least every twelve months to ensure the procedures are effective and have been complied with. The compliance procedures must be in writing except where there are fewer than ten individuals within the firm who are engaged in investment business. The firm must notify the Council in writing of the identity of those officers and employees who will conduct investment business in the practice year ending on 31 October following or within

1. Conduct of Investment Business Rules, r 3.3.

one month of a person becoming qualified in terms of the regulations[1]. However every officer of a certified person (that is every sole practitioner, partner or member of an incorporated practice) is responsible for ensuring compliance with the Conduct of Investment Business Rules and the Solicitors (Scotland) Investment Business Training Regulations, whether or not they personally conduct investment business[2].

The Council may require a certified person who acts as a discretionary portfolio manager to a significant extent (as to which the Council shall be the sole judge) to lodge a bond of caution in such form and for such sums as the Council may require. The Society would then call upon the bond of caution in the event of the insolvency of the certified person, and the sums paid under the bond would be applied by the Council in compensating any clients of the certified persons in proportion to the losses suffered by them as a result of the certified person's insolvency. At the time of writing the Council does not hold any bonds of caution and has recommended to SIB that this requirement can be dispensed with. Members of the Law Society of England and Wales have no similar requirement to lodge a bond of caution.

Hiving down

It is competent for solicitors' firms to set up stand-alone financial services companies which are not regulated by the Law Society in the conduct of investment business. However these hived-down financial service companies must be authorised by a self-regulating organisation (IMRO, PIA or SFA). The hived-down financial services company cannot be an appointed representative of another company.

The hived-down financial services company must be controlled by solicitors so that solicitors have a majority (but not necessarily a 100 per cent) shareholding and majority voting powers. The company must have a distinct and separate name

1. Solicitors (Scotland) Investment Business Training Regulations, r 4(a).
2. Ibid, r 4.1

from that of the solicitors as such as well as separate premises, a separate entrance and a separate nameplate[1]. In fact most solicitors derive their financial service business from their existing client base and there is every advantage for the solicitor in the client associating the company with the practice: as far as the solicitor is concerned, the particular advantages of the company lie in the limitation on claims for professional negligence which the company represents as well as the opportunity for enhanced fees.

1. Guidelines for the Establishment of Hived-off Financial Services Companies by Solicitors December 1993; Financial Services Company Guidance February 1994.

13. Money laundering

Money laundering offences

The Money Laundering Regulations 1993 which came into force on 1 April 1994, impose certain procedural requirements upon those conducting 'relevant financial businesses'. The purpose of the Regulations is to prevent the use of the financial system for the purpose of money laundering[1], and should be understood in the context of existing legislation which applies to all solicitors' business, irrespective of whether or not individual transactions fall within the ambit of the Money Laundering Regulations. Money laundering for the purposes of the Money Laundering Regulations means doing any act which constitutes an offence not only in relation to drug trafficking and drug money laundering but also in relation to prevention of terrorism and certain other criminal conduct. Certain additional offences, while not themselves amounting to money laundering, may be committed in relation to money laundering.

DRUG TRAFFICKING AND DRUG MONEY LAUNDERING

It is an offence under the Criminal Justice (International Co-operation) Act 1990, s 14 to conceal, disguise, convert or transfer from the jurisdiction property which represents the proceeds of drug trafficking (own funds money laundering). It is also an offence if, knowing or having reasonable grounds to suspect that any property represents another person's proceeds of drug trafficking, one conceals or disguises that property or removes it from the jurisdiction for the purpose of assisting any person to avoid a prosecution or the making or

---

1. Money Laundering Regulations 1993, preamble.

enforcement of a confiscation order. This includes the transfer of funds for the client intending to purchase property outwith the jurisdiction.

It is an offence under the Criminal Justice (Scotland) Act 1987, s 42A if, knowing or suspecting that any property in whole or in part directly or indirectly represents the proceeds of drug trafficking, a person acquires or uses that property or has possession of it. It is a defence to a charge of committing the offence that the person charged acquired or used the property or had possession of it for adequate consideration, which would ordinarily cover the application of funds to meet a solicitor's account, although presumably not if the fees were grossly excessive as the consideration would then be inadequate. However the provision of services which are of assistance to a person in terrorist-related activities are not to be treated as consideration, and it may be arguable whether the provision of legal services is 'of assistance' in terrorist-related activities. It would presumably be 'of assistance' if a terrorist were able to use the services of a solicitor to transfer funds out of the jurisdiction, since those funds could eventually be used for the purchase of arms or services.

A person is guilty of an offence under the Criminal Justice (Scotland) Act 1987, s 43 if, knowing or suspecting that another person is carrying on or has derived financial rewards from drug trafficking, that person enters into or is 'otherwise concerned in' an arrangement whereby retention or control of the proceeds of drug trafficking is facilitated. 'Knowing' may mean not only direct information but also circumstances which to persons of ordinary understanding and situated such as the accused must have led to the conclusion that the other person was a drug trafficker. Even if the circumstances do not warrant a finding of 'knowing' they may well warrant a finding of suspicion. It is suggested that there must be something more than a mere inkling or speculation but circumstances which might reasonably give rise to suspicion clearly include the use of large amounts of cash or other anonymous means of exchange, and may extend to the formal framework, for example use of advisors or nominees as directors or trustees with no apparent commercial involvement or the formation of companies or trusts with no apparent commercial purpose. Once suspicion is present, the taking of any step may be fraught with risk. Certainly the phrase 'concerned in' is sufficiently wide to include seemingly innocent transactions such as the purchase of property, shares or any moveables, whether in the UK or otherwise.

It is an offence under the Criminal Justice (Scotland) Act 1987, s 43A[1] if (a) knowing or suspecting that another person is engaged in drug money laundering and (b) that information or other matter on which suspicion is based comes to one's attention in the course of one's trade, profession, business or employment, (c) one does not then disclose the information to a constable or to a person commissioned by the Commissioners of Customs and Excise as soon as is reasonably practicable after it comes to one's attention.

It is not an offence for a professional legal adviser to fail to disclose any information or other matter which has come to him or her in privileged circumstances. However 'privileged circumstances' for the purposes of the Act is limited to matters concerning the giving of legal advice or information given in contemplation of, in connection with or for the purpose of legal proceedings. In England it has been held, in the context of discovery proceedings, that it is not necessary for a document to contain advice in order to be privileged, and legal privilege could extend to communications passing in the course of a conveyancing transaction: it was sufficient if the broad purpose of the communication was to obtain legal advice[2]. However privilege is unlikely to extend to business such as the financial arrangements for the sale and purchase of property, which is the area where most solicitors might expect to find evidence of or circumstances which might make them suspicious of money laundering. Further obligations and duties of disclosure are imposed by the Money Laundering Regulations, but it should be noted that the Criminal Justice (Scotland) Act 1987, s 43 applies even where a transaction is not caught by the Money Laundering Regulations, for example because the value is so small (although such a distinction is likely to be far more academic than real).

The Criminal Justice (Scotland) Act 1987, s 42(1) provides that a person who, knowing or suspecting that an investigation into drug trafficking is taking place, does anything which is

1. Inserted by the Criminal Justice Act 1993.
2. *Balabel v Air India* [1988] 2 All ER 246.

likely to prejudice the investigation is guilty of an offence. Unlike the provision for England and Wales, it is not necessary to show that there has been an application for a warrant for such material or grant of an order to make material available. An investigation is therefore protected even if it is at a very early stage, provided the accused knows or suspects its existence. It is for the accused to show that he or she did not know or suspect that what he or she did (which is not restricted to disclosure) was likely to prejudice the investigation. In Scotland it is also for the accused to show that he or she had no reasonable grounds to suspect that by acting as he or she did, this was likely to prejudice the investigation and it is suggested that the accused therefore has a harder task establishing a defence under this section in Scotland than in England and Wales.

PREVENTION OF TERRORISM

The Criminal Justice Act 1993, s 47 extends the offence of concealing or transferring the proceeds of terrorist-related activity to using or having possession of the relevant property, although it is a defence that the person charged acquired or used the property for adequate consideration. The section corresponds to the Criminal Justice (Scotland) Act 1987, s 42A.

The Criminal Justice Act 1993, s 49 amends the Prevention of Terrorism (Temporary Provisions) Act 1989 and creates an offence of using or possessing, whether for consideration or not, money or other property which represents the proceeds of terrorist-related activities. The Criminal Justice Act 1993, ss 50-51 creates similar offences in relation to terrorism as s 19 in relation to drug trafficking, that is offences of failure to disclose and of tipping off.

SERIOUS CRIMINAL CONDUCT

The Criminal Justice Act 1988, s 93A[1] makes it an offence to assist another to retain the benefits of criminal conduct. This is

---

1. The Criminal Justice Act 1993, s 33 inserted a new s 93E into the Criminal Justice Act 1988 which makes provision for the application to Scotland of the Criminal Justice Act 1988, ss 93A-93C.

a new departure and covers serious criminal conduct such as theft, burglary, blackmail and extortion. Section 93B mirrors s 42A making it an offence to acquire or use property which is known to be derived in whole or in part from someone else's serious criminal conduct. The same defences are available; such as that the property was acquired for adequate consideration or that suspicions were disclosed to the appropriate person. Section 93C creates an offence of concealing or transferring the proceeds of serious criminal conduct in order to avoid or assist another to avoid prosecution. For the purposes of s 93C (as for the Criminal Justice (International Co-operation) Act 1990, s 14 which it mirrors) it is sufficient if the defender had reasonable grounds to suspect the criminal origin of the proceeds. Finally s 93D creates an offence of tipping off.

Money laundering regulations

GENERAL

As noted above, the requirements of existing legislation means that it is already an offence for any person to provide assistance to a money launderer or prejudice any investigation by disclosure. However, non-compliance with the Money Laundering Regulations constitutes a separate statutory offence whether or not money laundering has taken place[1]. In addition, non-compliance for solicitors constitutes professional misconduct.

The Money Laundering Regulations 1993[2] apply to any business arrangement or relationship which is carried out 'in the course of relevant financial business'. From the point of view of solicitors, relevant financial business includes investment business within the meaning of the Financial Services Act 1986[3] but the Solicitors (Scotland) Accounts Rules 1995 go further and require firms to comply with the regulations whether or not the firm carries out relevant financial business. The

---

1. Reg 5.
2. Which came into force on 1 April 1994.
3. Money Laundering Regulations, reg 4.

amendments are intended to extend to all relevant client funds, whatever their source or destination.

Where the offence is committed by a partnership failing to comply with the regulations and where this is committed with the consent or 'attributable to any neglect on the part of the partner . . . he as well as the partnership . . . shall be guilty of that offence and shall be liable to be proceeded against and punished accordingly'.

In terms of the regulations, solicitors are required to maintain (1) identification procedures; (2) record keeping procedures; (3) internal reporting procedures; (4) such other internal procedures as may be appropriate.

IDENTIFICATION PROCEDURES

Verification of identity is not normally needed in the case of a single one-off transaction, when payment by or to the applicant is less than ECU 15,000 (say, £12,000). However, it would not be wise to rely on this exemption since if it appears either at the outset or in any later stage that the transactions are linked and the aggregate amount is ECU 15,000 or more, the verification procedures should be undertaken. Where evidence of identity is required it must be obtained at the earliest stage at which there are reasonable grounds for believing the total amount payable is ECU 15,000 or more. Regulation 7 (1) requires that where the evidence is not obtained 'the business relationship or one off transaction in question shall not proceed any further'.

This means that in certain circumstances the firm may have to freeze a transaction at a critical stage. In preparing their procedures, firms need to form a commercial view as to the likelihood of this happening and as to how they will freeze the transaction if it does. For investment business the official guidelines suggest this may mean freezing the right attaching to an investment after dealing before settlement or delivery. This situation could be even more critical for solicitors since the regulations extend to compliance with the Accounts Rules generally and may lead to severe difficulties if the solicitor requires to decide whether or not evidence is satisfactory at a delicate stage in negotiations, say just before expiry of time limits for acceptance of an offer or lodging of licensing applications, planning appeals, or before delivery of a certified copy of a newly created charge to the Companies Register. The consequences for the new client of non-compliance with these limits could be enormous, and it may be difficult to argue convincingly that the solicitor was justified in freezing the transaction if this could have been averted by taking adequate instructions in terms of the verification procedures at the outset.

For these reasons, it is suggested that it is prudent to maintain identification procedures in respect of all clients from the outset. It should be noted that irrespective of the size and nature of transactions and any exemptions, identity must be verified in all cases where money laundering is known or suspected[1]. Although verification may sound onerous, much of the information should be obtained by the prudent solicitor at the outset of any transaction, whether covered by the Money Laundering Regulations or not. Failure to verify, say, the exact designation or authority of partners of a company, may have serious repercussions in any context.

Verification procedures should deal with the following category of applicants for business.

(1) Clients paying by post or electronic transfer

Where payment is to be made by the applicant and it is reasonable for payment to be sent by post or effective electronic means, the fact that payment is debited from an account held in the applicant's name at an authorised bank or European authorised institution or authorised credit institution is capable of constituting the required evidence of identity.

In this case, a record should be made of (a) branch sorting code; (b) the account number; (c) name and address of the appropriate institutions; and (d) when the cheque or payment is made, it should be confirmed that there is no inconsistency between the name in which the application is made and the name on the cheque.

Although this sounds very straightforward, it may present practical difficulties if, as noted above, a transaction requires to be frozen at a delicate stage simply because the evidence

1. Money Laundering Regulations 1993, r 7(3).

which was capable of constituting the required evidence of identity becomes no longer capable of being relied upon, because of the inconsistency. Again, in the circumstances, it seems more prudent to use this as supplementary information, but it is wise to insist upon independent verification procedure from the outset.

(2) UK registered corporate applicants

Where the applicant is an unquoted company or a partnership, the solicitor should:

(a) Identify one or more of the principals, directors/partners and/or shareholders if not already known.
(b) Obtain latest report and accounts (audited where applicable).
(c) Obtain a copy Certificate of Incorporation.
(d) If there is any uncertainty it may be prudent to make a credit reference agency search or take a banker's reference. An agency search is instructed directly by the solicitor but at the firm's cost (unless passed on to the client). A banker's reference requires co-operation of the clients, and the bank would charge the client.

It is suggested that there is no need to make further investigation where the applicant is a quoted company, but it is prudent to verify the authority of a director or authorised signatory. In many cases this is covered by the requirement to obtain minutes of the board of directors or shareholders' meetings authorising major transactions such as acquisitions, but these minutes are not available at the outset of a transaction.

(3) UK resident personal applicants for business including partnerships

The following information should be obtained and should be independently verified:

(a) True name and all names used.
(b) Current permanent address including postcode. There are various suggestions for verification including a visit to the home of an applicant and checking a telephone directory (although this only gives the initial not the full name).

Perhaps the most practicable is 'a current valid full passport or national identity card' or if that is unacceptable a current driving licence.

(c) For a partnership, the solicitor should obtain evidence that the parties are indeed in partnership together and designated partners have authority to bind the partnership for the transaction in question. In some cases the partnership deed is exhibited but if the parties do not wish to disclose details of internal financial arrangements such as division of profit, a letter of confirmation is sufficient.

(4) Non-UK resident personal applicants

Business is likely to be conducted by post or telephone. Verification of identity should be sought from a reputable institution or a professional advisor known to the firm in the applicant's country of residence.

It is suggested that the applicant should be asked to produce a letter of introduction from a local solicitor.

(5) Non-UK registered companies

Non-UK registered companies have comparable requirements to UK resident companies. In addition, verification of the identity of at least one of the individuals concerned by letter of introduction from a local firm of solicitors should be obtained.

(6) Institutional investors

No exceptional inquiries are required where the applicant is a development agency or local authority or pension fund of a limited company.

For English charities, check charitable status with the Registrar of Charities in England. For Scottish charities, check with the Inland Revenue. In each case it is prudent to request a copy of the Trust Deed and copies of the deed of appointment of trustees or some other confirmation as to the trustees' status. For other pension funds it is suggested that the solicitor check the relevant industry directory but again verification of trustees' status is prudent.

(7) Agents

Where an intermediary deals in its own name as an agent for its own client (as opposed to merely introducing him or her) it is the intermediary which is the applicant for business and not its client. This includes solicitors who instruct correspondents on behalf of their client, and solicitors in turn should expect to have to comply with identification procedures where they have instructed agents on behalf of clients.

The Regulations require that the firm must in addition verify the identity of the underlying client.

Where the applicants for business are regulated by an overseas regulatory authority, it is reasonable to accept a written assurance from the applicant to the effect that evidence of the identity of the principal has been obtained and recorded on the procedures maintained by the applicant's business. In other circumstances (for example UK solicitors) solicitors are required to take 'reasonable measures'. In this case, it is certainly reasonable to simply require a written assurance that evidence of the identity of the principal has been obtained and recorded by the principal.

GENERAL

In practical terms most firms are likely to find that it is sufficient to create a pro forma checklist for new clients and retain this within the client file. Firms may wish to transfer the information to their own database but this is not necessary. Completion of a pro forma checklist, however, in this as in all other areas is no substitute for the solicitor using his or her professional judgment. If a client is unwilling to provide the information requested the solicitor should ask why. Whether the failure to provide information is sufficient to ground suspicion is open to debate, but the failure to inquire is certainly a breach of the Regulations.

RECORD-KEEPING PROCEDURES

The requirement to verify identity is not retrospective and applies only to new one-off transactions and business relationships entered into after 1 April 1994. Once identification procedures have been satisfactorily completed, then as long as records are maintained, no further evidence is needed and subsequent transactions are undertaken. Note, however, the requirement to maintain internal reporting procedures.

Where evidence of identity is obtained by or on behalf of the client, the solicitor must retain a record that (a) indicates the nature of the evidence; (b) comprises a copy of the evidence (or such information as enables a copy to be obtained or reobtained); (c) details all transactions carried out by the applicant in the course of relevant financial business.

The prescribed period is at least five years commencing with (a) completion of the relevant business; (b) date of the last transaction if formalities necessary to end a business relationship have not been observed; (c) taking any steps for the purposes of recovering all or part of the debt payable by an applicant after it is believed that the applicant has become insolvent.

As the Law Society guidelines recommend retention of most records for ten years, the five-year cut-off should not cause any problems. However, the solicitor should consider whether a separate register should be retained or whether (as seems likely) the information can be retrieved in the context of existing retention and retrieval procedures.

INTERNAL REPORTING PROCEDURES

It is up to the solicitor's firm to devise its own internal recording procedures, but these are in accordance with the regulations if they include the following provisions:

(1) identifying the appropriate person to whom the report is to be made of any suspicion that another person is engaged in money laundering ('the Money Laundering Officer');

(2) requiring that any such report be considered in light of all other relevant information by the appropriate persons (or by another designated person);

(3) the person charged with considering the report in accordance with (2) has reasonable access to other information which may be of assistance; and

(4) securing that the information contained in the report is

disclosed to a constable (which includes a person commissioned by the Commissioners of Customs and Excise).

It is not sufficient to simply maintain that the procedures are understood. They should be formally recorded, by inclusion in an office manual.

Regulation 5 of the Money Laundering Regulations requires firms to take appropriate measures to make relevant employees aware of the policies and procedures and to provide these employees with training in recognition of handling suspicious transactions. The Regulations do not specify the nature of the training, but might include:

(1) circulation of these notes or inclusion in an office manual;
(2) appointment of a Money Laundering Officer;
(3) annual review.

THE SOLICITOR'S DUTY

In normal circumstances the solicitor has a duty to keep the affairs of a client confidential and should ensure that staff do the same. However the legislation and Money Laundering Regulations combine to replace that duty with a duty of disclosure in certain circumstances. Failure to disclose is a criminal offence while the fact of disclosure, contrary to the accepted norms, provides a defence to the criminal offence and to a claim for IPS and/or negligence or breach of contract by a client. Accordingly if the solicitor has any suspicion then this should be reported to the investigating authority even though, by doing so, the solicitor is in breach of the normal duty of confidentiality to the client. The solicitor may also be required to breach client confidentiality if required to do so by order of the court, for example a warrant issued to the Serious Fraud Office under the Criminal Justice Act 1987, s 2.

In normal circumstances, the solicitor also has a duty not to mislead the client, and to be 'frank and open with the client' and to keep the client 'fully informed in relation to the transaction in which the solicitor is engaged on behalf of the client, particularly if any difficulty arises'[1]. Again this duty may be

1. Tribunal decision 822/91.

replaced with a duty to conceal certain matters from the client, so there is no tipping off. Having disclosed suspicions to the appropriate authorities, a solicitor may be authorised and indeed instructed to proceed with a transaction.

The duty to deal with a client's affairs without undue delay is displaced by the requirements not to proceed further if the solicitor does not obtain the necessary verification under the Money Laundering Regulations and not to proceed with a transaction which would constitute an offence in terms of the legislation or the Regulations.

14. Complaints and discipline

Accountability

The solicitor has always been liable to account to the client but developments in consumer law and confidence over the last 20 years have meant that the modern solicitor is more directly accountable to the client than ever before. This includes not merely financial accounting for funds held, but accounting for time spent on behalf of the client. These principles are reinforced by the detailed Accounts Rules considered in chapter 11 and the rules relating to fee charging considered in chapter 10.

The solicitor is obliged to account to third parties where there has been negligence, and also accounts to professional colleagues in the sense that each solicitor is subject to the disciplinary powers and procedures of the Law Society and, ultimately, of the Discipline Tribunal. As this book attempts to demonstrate, a solicitor may be disciplined not simply for failing to deliver a service to clients but for infringing professional standards, whether written or unwritten.

Complaints to the practice

The Law Society has developed a formal machinery for handling complaints against solicitors, but has recognised that the vast majority of complaints by clients relate to deficiencies in the quality of service by solicitors rather than more extreme professional misconduct. What most clients are looking for is a speedy resolution of their particular grievance, rather than a prolonged investigation and disciplinary measures against the solicitor which may not address their particular problem. The Law Society has therefore placed the emphasis very firmly upon conciliation rather than confrontation, and stresses that wherever possible any complaint should be dealt with by the practice itself, which should develop its own complaints handling machinery[1].

It is suggested that each practice appoints a complaints or client relations partner who should take responsibility for dealing with all complaints (although any complaints against that partner should in turn be handled by another partner). Practical guidelines for practices, as set out in the Law Society's guidance manual, are reproduced as Appendix 5.

Complaints to the Law Society

Complaints which cannot be resolved in this way may eventually be considered by one of the Law Society's three Complaints Committees whose membership is made up of Council members, other practising solicitors and independent lay members. In keeping with the emphasis on conciliation, one of the deputy secretaries first tries to resolve the matter by attempting informal dispute resolution to resolve the complaint without invoking the more formal procedures which may lead to consideration by the Committee. Inevitably some complaints cannot be resolved in this way and, even where the client is satisfied, it is still open for a complaint to be referred to a Committee to formally consider any instance which amounts to professional misconduct or unprofessional conduct.

Where the conduct complained of is sufficiently serious the Committee may recommend to Council that the solicitor concerned should be prosecuted for professional misconduct before the Discipline Tribunal. Where Council accepts that recommendation, the matter is referred to the Society's fiscal for preparation of the appropriate complaint and the fiscal is responsible for conduct of the proceedings before the Tribunal. The Committee may decide that, although the conduct complained of amounts to professional misconduct, this warrants a reprimand rather than a prosecution. The issue of a reprimand

---

1. For an authoritative summary of the new complaints philosophy and procedure see RG Christie 'Complaints against solicitors' 1994 JLSS 43.

forms part of a solicitor's disciplinary record, and before a formal decision is taken the solicitor is advised that the matter is being treated as an allegation of misconduct and that the solicitor has the right to attend an interview or to make written representations. If the solicitor does not accept the issue of the reprimand, the issue may then be referred to the Tribunal. In practice it is fair to say that almost all solicitors who accept they have been guilty of professional misconduct accept the issue of the reprimand as a preferable alternative to reference to the Discipline Tribunal, not simply in terms of expense but also bearing in mind that a reprimand does not attract mandatory publicity, as a reference to the Tribunal usually does.

Where a Committee considers the conduct is not so serious, it may make a finding of unprofessional conduct and issue a letter indicating that the Society either deplores or regrets the conduct which is the subject of the complaint. A letter in these terms does not form part of the disciplinary record of the solicitor. Where the Council is satisfied that it is necessary for the purpose of investigating a complaint made to it or remitted to it by the Tribunal, the Council may require the solicitor to produce or deliver all documents for examination and provide an explanation within a stated period regarding the matters to which the complaint relates[1]. Apart from the complaint at issue, it is also professional misconduct on the part of the solicitor to delay or fail to respond to correspondence from the Council in relation to the complaint or any other matter. Experience has shown that when solicitors encounter personal or professional difficulties this is reflected in a series of complaints from clients of delay and failure to communicate, and the delay extends to the solicitor's dealings with the Law Society. The Council has therefore to use at least the threat of a s42C notice more often than one might expect.

As already noted, the Society now has the power to make a finding of inadequate professional service in terms of the Solicitors (Scotland) Act 1980, s 42A. Where the Council has made such a finding under s 42A(1) it may take such steps mentioned in s 42A(2) as it thinks fit. This includes not only the power to reduce fees to nil but also to order the solicitor's firm to

---

1. Solicitors (Scotland) Act 1980, s 42C.

rectify any error or other deficiency or take such action at its own expense as the Council may specify. The cost might be considerable as it is theoretically possible to require the firm to, say, undertake extensive conveyancing or even litigation at its own expense. If the effect of an order was disproportionately harsh it is open to an aggrieved solicitor to appeal to the Discipline Tribunal in terms of s 42A. However actual compensation payable to the complainer is limited to £1,000 and in practise the Council has been fairly conservative in making orders under this section. Unless a complainer indicates that a negligence claim has been intimated or an action commenced, the question of adequacy of service can be considered as set out in s 56A of the 1980 Act but clients who have suffered significant losses are likely to advance a claim for professional negligence against the solicitor, effectively leaving the matter to be dealt with by insurers and the court rather than the Council. The effect of s 42A in practice is therefore almost like a small claims court in that it provides a mechanism for the client to recover fees or minimal compensation from the solicitor for defective service. Unfortunately the availability of s 42A, like all litigation, is also open to abuse by clients who are aware of the nuisance value inherent in any complaint. There is a real concern that scarce Council resources are being diverted into consideration of relatively trivial matters which could not be warranted in terms of any cost benefit analysis, hence the encouragement of conciliation wherever possible which, even if it does not succeed, will highlight the outstanding problem areas.

Where the Committee knows at the time of making its decision that the solicitor complained of has been sequestrated, it makes a formal determination to the effect that IPS had been provided and compensation would have been appropriate but as no decision could be implemented, normally no compensation order will be made.

Complaints before the Discipline Tribunal

Where the Council considers that the conduct complained of is sufficiently serious, it recommends prosecution before the Discipline Tribunal set up under the 1980 Act, s 50. The Tribunal has jurisdiction to hear any complaints of professional misconduct, including any case where it appears that a solicitor has been seeking to make extraordinary and apparently unjustified claims against a client or the Scottish Legal Aid Board[1]. It may also consider the question of the standard of service provided.

Complaints to the Tribunal are normally made by the Council after going through the procedures outlined above, but may also be made by the Lord Advocate, any judge, the Dean of the Faculty of Advocates, the Auditor of the Court of Session or any sheriff court, the Scottish Legal Aid Board or the Scottish Legal Services Ombudsman[2]. The powers of the Tribunal are set out in the 1980 Act, s 53 and Schedule 4 and include the power to strike off, suspend the solicitor from practice or from exercising a right of audience and a power to impose a fine of up to £10,000. All fines are forfeit to the Crown but the Tribunal may make an award of expenses incurred by the other party or by the Tribunal against either complainer or respondent. These costs can be significant, outweighing any fine. In addition, the respondent has to face the burden of publicity given to most decisions[3] although the Tribunal may refrain from publishing names, places or other facts which would in its opinion damage or be likely to damage the interests of the solicitor against whom the complaint was made or his or her partners or any of their families[4].

A definitive account of the Tribunal, its procedure and decisions has been written by John Barton, Clerk to the Tribunal for 20 years, in association with the Law Society[5].

Guarantee Fund

The Guarantee Fund was originally established by the Solicitors (Scotland) Act 1948, re-enacted as the 1980 Act, s 43. The Fund is vested in the Society and is under the control of management of the Council. Every solicitor is required to pay

1. 1980 Act, s 50(2).
2. Ibid, s 51(3).
3. Ibid, Sch 4, para 14.
4. Ibid, Sch 4, para 14A.
5. Smith and Barton *Procedures and Decisions of the Scottish Solicitors' Discipline Tribunal* (1995, T&T Clark).

an annual contribution to the Society on behalf of the Guarantee Fund, while incorporated practices pay an annual corporate contribution calculated by reference to the number of solicitors who are directors or employees of the incorporated practice[1]. The amount of the contribution required depends on the claims made on the Guarantee Fund, and regrettably has risen over the years as a result of an increase in both the number and value of claims.

The Act directs the Society to hold the Guarantee Fund 'for the purpose of making grants in order to compensate persons who in the opinion of the Council suffer pecuniary loss by reason of dishonesty' on the part of a solicitor or any employee of a solicitor, whether or not the solicitor had a practising certificate in force at the time the dishonesty was committed and whether or not the solicitor may have subsequently died, or been removed, suspended or struck off the roll of solicitors. However grants are not available in respect of losses which have arisen while the solicitor was suspended from practice, as opposed to suspended subsequent to the commission of the act of dishonesty[2]. Although the Society attempts to deal with claims as quickly as possible, the fact is that by the time most claims are adjudicated upon and paid, any solicitor responsible for the dishonesty has probably long since been disciplined and it is more than likely he or she is no longer practising as a solicitor.

Most cases giving rise to claims on the Guarantee Fund are caused by shortages on the client account of sole practitioners, and two and three partner firms. This is not because sole practitioners are fundamentally dishonest, but because the cover available under the mandatory Master Policy for professional indemnity insurance includes not only negligence but also fidelity cover where there is a shortage on clients' funds, provided there is at least one innocent partner. That fidelity cover is, by definition, not available to sole practitioners who have no partners, innocent or otherwise, and consequently any claims for dishonesty against a sole practitioner are bound to fall against the Guarantee Fund. The Council may refuse to

1. Solicitors (Scotland)Act 1980, Sch 3.
2. Ibid, s 43(3)(b).

make a grant, or may make a limited grant if it is of the opinion that there has been negligence on the part of any person for whom the claimant is responsible which has contributed to the loss in question[1].

Losses which can be made good otherwise, for example through a claim on the Master Policy, or from assets of the principals of the practice, may not be paid from the Guarantee Fund[2]. In practice, where it is clear that the Fund will be required to make some payment at the end of the day, the Society has been prepared to meet claims directly out of the Fund and then recover from the solicitor principals where possible, rather than require a claimant to first exhaust all legal remedies. In making any payment the Society takes an assignation of all claims, so that it may pursue any legal remedies to enforce payment. This may include pursuing a claim for negligence against the firm's accountants, either in right of the claimant or in its own right. It may also include making solicitor principals bankrupt in the absence of adequate insurance and/or assets.

Enforcement through the courts

Where there has been professional negligence, the claimant is entitled to intimate a claim against the solicitor's firm and its professional indemnity insurers and, ultimately, to pursue that claim through the courts if no satisfactory settlement is reached. All solicitors are required to have in place professional indemnity insurance as a precondition of the issue of a practising certificate. Since 1 November 1978 there has been in place a mandatory scheme for minimal insurance (currently £1,000,000) effected through a Master Policy, underwritten by the commercial insurance market. Lead insurers and claims handlers are Sun Alliance, who maintain an in-house team of claims handlers but refer more difficult claims to a panel of appointed solicitors with particular experience in professional negligence claims.

1. 1980 Act, s 43(5).
2. Ibid, s 43(3)(a).

Quis custodiet custodes?

Where a complainer considers that the Law Society has not dealt with his or her complaint adequately, the matter may be referred to the Legal Services Ombudsman, successor to the former Lay Observer[1]. The Legal Services Ombudsman is appointed by the Secretary of State after consultation with the Lord President and has jurisdiction to examine any written complaint made by or on behalf of a member of the public concerning the Society's handling of a complaint. This is without prejudice to a complainer's right to pursue any legal remedy including the right to apply to the court in the ordinary way for judicial review of any administrative decision. Thus disaffected claimants on the Guarantee Fund have from time to time threatened to apply for judicial review of the refusal to make an award, although there has not yet been any successful appplication.

The Legal Services Ombudsman is required to make such investigation of the complaint as seems appropriate and in this context may request the Society to provide him or her with such information as may be reasonably required. In practice this means that the Ombudsman usually calls for examination of the Law Society's own files, including Committee and Council minutes, and the Society is obliged to furnish the information requested[2]. After investigation, the Ombudsman may refer an individual complaint back to the Law Society with a recommendation for review. The Ombudsman has no power of enforcement as such, although the Society is required to consider any report which the Ombudsman issues and to notify the Ombudsman of any action which it has taken in consequence[3], and the Ombudsman has the power to refer a matter directly to the Tribunal, which does have effective sanctions[4]. The Ombudsman also publishes an annual report, analysing the referred cases and making general recommendations to the Society for future handling and disposal of complaints.

1. Law Reform (Miscellaneous Provisions) (Scotland) Act 1990, s 34.
2. Ibid, Sch 3, para 7.
3. Ibid, Sch 3, para 8.
4. 1980 Act, s 51(3)(f).

15. Assistance for the solicitor

The vast majority of complaints against solicitors arise out of delay or failure to communicate. The failure to attend to clients' affairs can arise from any number of reasons, particularly overwork, poor management and office systems and purely personal difficulties. As ever, prevention is better than cure and proper management systems and allocation of work can do much to relieve the strain on individual solicitors and to ensure an efficient service to clients.

Solicitors should expect to enjoy the support of their partners or employers and should feel able to approach partners or employers when any individual case or an accumulation of problems begins to assume alarming proportions. An internal disciplinary regime should not exist in isolation from a framework for grievance and constructive support of all staff, including partners.

In some circumstances however the solicitor may not feel able to approach his or her partners, for instance if worried about the finances of the firm, or for purely personal reasons. Partners and particularly sole practioners may find it difficult to informally approach solicitors in another firm who, although colleagues, are also their professional competitors and this may extend to a reluctance to speak to their local Council member. The Law Society itself offers a counselling service and makes available a senior practitioner, who is not local to the area and who will attend at least two interviews free of charge to the solicitor. Alternative sources of advice include the Legal Defence Union, which not only advises but represents a member in disciplinary hearings, whether before the Law Society, the Tribunal or the courts.

Finally, solicitors as well as their clients should consider formal professional advice. 'It is never too early to call your solicitor' is sound advice for all clients, who in 1995 can look to their solicitor for standards of professionalism and service as high, if not higher, than they have ever been.

Appendices

Examples of conflicts of interest in commercial security transactions*

The following illustrate some of the instances where lenders and borrowers have separate interests in commercial security transactions.

1. Disclosure of all relevant circumstances

Either:
(a) the solicitor may know more of the borrower's position than has been communicated to the lender or *vice versa*; or
(b) there may have been a reluctance by the borrower or lender fully to disclose their respective positions because of dual representation.

This clearly affects the extent to which impartial 'best advice' can be given.

2. Ongoing negotiations

Negotiations between the borrower and lender may have only reached the 'Outline Terms' stage – requiring further detailed consideration or negotiation of covenants/undertakings/events of default. In such negotiations the borrower and lender may have different negotiating strengths – and thus there may be competing pressures on the solicitor as to whose interests are to be promoted.

3. Defects in title

While a borrower may be prepared to 'live with' a minor defect in title or some lack of planning or building consent the lender may take an entirely different stance.

4. Security by companies

Apart from the complexities and time restraints for registration of security; companies may well be subject to negative or restrictive covenants or powers affecting the security on which the borrower but not necessarily the lender, may be prepared to take a commercial view. This may merit separate consideration and advice.

5. Competing creditors/ranking agreements

The circumstances as to the inter-relationship/enforcement of security

* Letter issued by the President of the Law Society, 15.2.1994.

between lenders may merit separate consideration and advice. Banks may not have 'standard forms' of ranking agreements and this clearly may involve a solicitor in preparing a document and negotiating its terms on points which have a bearing on the borrower's position.

6. Security over commercial property

The permitted use, associated licences/quotas and specific standard conditions may merit separate consideration and advice as they may not be covered by pre-printed 'standard' bank forms. Particular risks arise on the transfer of a licence where the lender's interests will sometimes conflict with the borrower's commercial ambitions.

7. Leased property as security

The circumstances in which a lender requires protection in the event of irritancy may merit separate consideration and advice. Invariably the borrower is trying to strike the best deal while he is in occupancy while the lender needs protection in the event of the borrower's failure through insolvency or otherwise.

8. Enforcement of security

The solicitor acting for both borrower and lender may be placed in difficulty in the event of subsequent enforcement of a security. For whom does the solicitor act in such circumstances? Do both clients know and understand their respective positions?

9. Powerful clients

A major business client may bring subtle or even open pressures on a solicitor to follow a particular course or to turn a blind eye to a matter which could prejudice a lender's position eg discrepancies between a valuation and purchase price.

10. All sums due: securities

Solicitors should be mindful to advise fully, joint obligants (husbands and wives) of the nature of an 'all sums due' security. In particular it should be drawn to their attention that additional loans for example in respect of one obligant's business, may give rise to further secured borrowings without the other obligant requiring to sign the documentation.

11. Companies – *ultra vires*

Following changes to the *ultra vires* doctrine lenders may be able to rely on the provisions of what is now section 35 of the 1985 Companies Act.

   If the solicitors involved act solely for the lender they would, as a generality, be entitled to rely on these same provisions if asked to do so by the instructing lender. On the other hand if the solicitors act also for the borrowing company it is quite clear that the solicitors would require to carry out a full examination of the company's Memorandum and Articles of Association, since section 35 only provides protection for third parties – it does not for example excuse the directors from any liability arising from acting ultra vires. In such circumstances the solicitors, as agents for the lender, would become aware of any ultra vires aspect of the arrangements and the lender could be similarly tainted with this knowledge.

Law Society table of fees for conveyancing and general business

APPENDIX. GUIDELINES ON CHARGING ACCORDING TO CIRCUMSTANCES

The General Regulations for transactions charged according to circumstances are contained in paragraphs 4 and 5 of Chapter 1 hereof and all Solicitors should be thoroughly familiar with these paragraphs. Some amplification of these paragraphs will be found in these guidelines. The guidelines are intended to assist in a practical way those Solicitors who find it difficult, in the absence of a recommended scale or percentage fee, to arrive at a fair and reasonable fee charged according to circumstances.

The Council advances the following guidelines.

1. It is an overriding principle in fee charging that a Solicitor's fee should be fair and reasonable to both himself and his client. No two cases are identical. The rate for the job is flexible and adaptable and takes into account all relevant factors in each case.

2. The fixing of every fee is a balanced judgment rather than an arithmetical calculation and the Solicitor has to apply his judgment to the fixing of every fee. In charging according to circumstances a Solicitor will not necessarily be charging the same fee as another for the same work. Fees which are unreasonably high would not be upheld in a taxation and may amount to professional misconduct. At the other extreme, every Solicitor has a responsibility to ensure that the fees he charges are sufficient to enable the work to be carried out to the proper professional standard. Failure to discharge that responsibility may amount to professional misconduct. Within the range of reasonableness the fee will vary from one transaction to another and may vary from one Solicitor to another. The Solicitor will require to be able to justify his fee not only to the client but to an auditor in a taxation.

3. It is highly desirable for two reasons that a Solicitor should keep as detailed records as possible in respect of the work carried out for his client. First, it will enable the Solicitor to ascertain the total amount of his or his assistant's time which has been incurred in any transaction. He will almost certainly find this helpful in charging appropriate fees. Second, if a taxation of fees is called for, the Solicitor will be asked to justify his fee and he may require to identify each item of charge by an entry or series of entries on the client's file.

4. The Solicitor's fee may consist of charges for detailed items and other calculable elements not new to the Profession, that is, letters, telephone calls, meetings (including travelling time), perusal and drafting of documents etc. These may be charged at the current unit rate recommended by the General Table of Fees. The unit rate contains a modest allowance for supplementary factors as mentioned in General Regulation 4 and any further weighting for such factors in a normal case would require to be carefully considered.

5. Charging solely for detailed items as in paragraph 4 above is not the normal practice for transactions involving conveyances and leases for value. In such transactions the auditor will generally allow a charge which relates in some way to the value of the transaction. For such transactions it would be normal practice to charge according to circumstances with an important element in the circumstances being the value of the transaction. Reference is made to paragraph 4 and 5 of the General Regulations. Generally the logical starting-point in the charging process is the time expended, but in some cases the relevance of one or more of the other factors set out in General Regulation 4 may substantially outweigh the time factor and the charge may not bear a direct relationship to the time expended. This will normally be the case in transactions involving conveyances and leases for value. The rate charged should take into account all seven factors in the General Regulations and also the amount of any hourly rate applied to time expended.

6. It is important to establish an hourly charge rate for each fee earner whether a principal or staff member. It is most desirable that before setting such hourly charge rate, the expense of doing the work should first be determined by some suitable method. The Law Society of Scotland has published a helpful booklet *The Cost of Time* which can be obtained at a small cost. Participation in the Cost of Time Surveys which the Society undertakes will also be of considerable assistance. Substantial regard should then be given to such expense rate or cost of time in setting an hourly charge rate. If hourly charge rates are fixed without reference to the costs of running a practice, the hourly charge rates may be quite divorced from such costs, and may as a consequence be unfair either to the practitioner or to the client. The setting of an hourly charge rate for each fee earner is the basic structure that should be put in place for each practice before charging an individual transaction can proceed.

7. Once hourly charge rates have been set, the first step in charging a particular transaction is to determine the product of the hourly charge rate, and the time expended. An appraisal of the resultant figure should then be made to see whether the expense is reasonable from the point of view of the client. For example, the time taken may have been excessive or the grade of fee earner who performed the work may have been more senior than was appropriate. On the other hand, the time expended may have been less than would normally be expected, having regard to the efficient manner in which the work was carried out. Any appropriate adjustment should then be made. This, then, represents the time and labour factor of the remuneration and takes into account the reasonable costs of running your practice.

8. The charge to be made may well contain an element which reflects all other relevant factors, and more particularly the remaining factors set out in General Regulation 4 of the Table of Fees. These remaining factors combined with the time and labour factor together provide, in the normal case, a basis for assessing the fairness and reasonableness of the charge proposed to be made. The extent to which the other relevant factors will affect the time and labour factor of the remuneration will to a large degree be governed by the hourly charge rate of the particular fee earner. For example, if the hourly charge rate is high, then less weighting would occur under the item of skill, specialised knowledge and responsibility required, as a fee earner with a high hourly charge rate would normally be expected to undertake work demanding skill, specialised knowledge and responsibility.

9. There may be factors which produce a negative weighting, eg, (a) the property involved is of very small value, or (b) the work carried out is of a particularly routine or straightforward nature. If in any of such cases a downward adjustment is already made out as previously indicated in calculating the time and labour factor of the remuneration, this may in itself produce a fair and reasonable fee without further adjustment by applying the foregoing factors.

10. Finally, the practitioner should step back and take an overall view of the transaction as a whole to check whether the fee arrived at by the above process is fair and reasonable. This final appraisal should be carried out not only from the viewpoint of the practitioner but also from that of a reasonable client. In some cases, this final appraisal will result in a downwards adjustment on the basis that the job simply will not stand the fee arrived at. On the other hand, there will be occasions when the fee can be adjusted upwards on this final appraisal. It is again stressed that the ultimate test of the appropriate charge to be made in each case is whether it is fair and reasonable and the practitioner must accept the responsibility for determining what is the fair and reasonable charge to be made in the particular circumstances of the case, having regard to the criteria set out in General Regulations 4.

11. The Council recognises that a Solicitor, once he acquires experience of charging on the foregoing basis, may find, for transactions which are fairly typical and which involve no more and no less than the normal amount of work, that he wishes to create his own table of fees for such transactions, particularly with a view to providing quotations and estimates of fees for clients prior to commencing the work. The Council has no objections to such as proposal provided that the Solicitor always applies to the fee fixed in any transaction the ultimate test of whether it is fair and reasonable. It will be for each practice to develop this approach on their own initiative but the following views have emerged in consultation with the Profession for normal domestic property transactions.

(*a*) A Solicitor's time and work involved in a sale is about four-fifths of the time and work involved in a purchase, eg, taking units as six minutes of time: 50 units for a purchase, 40 units for a sale to which may be added some weighting for value, or

(*b*) the fee may be a percentage charge of say 1 per cent on a purchase and 0.8 per cent on a sale plus, where applicable, a fee for missives, or

(*c*) where a Solicitor is entitled to charge commission on sale, the fee may be a percentage charge on the sale price which is fully inclusive of commission on sale and fees for missives and conveyancing.

12. In cases inducing a first registration in terms of the Land Registration (Scotland) Act 1979 some additional weighting will normally be appropriate in respect of the length, number and importance of the documents prepared or perused, but for dealings in a registered interest, a negative weighting will be appropriate.

13. In considering the application of a value or supplementary factor in the feeing of work involving security deeds, leases and other matters to which conveyancing scale fees no longer apply the following views are advanced.

(a) In the variation, restriction or discharge of security deeds a value or supplementary factor should not normally be charged. In the constitution of security deeds, where the Solicitor is acting in such matters for the lender and the borrower and is also acting for the borrower as the purchaser of the security subjects, any value or supplementary factor to be applied should take into account the value or supplementary factor already included in the fee for the conveyance.

(b) In preparation of leases and subsidiary writs, any value or supplementary factor may be based on the total sum exigible under the contract or during the first ten years thereof, whichever is less.

14. It is accepted that before embarking on business involving the sale or purchase of property, the inquirer is entitled to know the approximate cost in fees and outlays. A Solicitor may have formulated his own table of fees in which case he will be able to quote from the table. Otherwise it will be necessary for the Solicitor to inform the inquirer that until the transaction has been completed his fee for the work involved cannot be accurately quoted in advance. However, he may be in a position to inform the inquirer initially that the fee will fall within a range of two figures thus providing the inquirer with a minimum and maximum figure. A Solicitor should make it clear in all cases that if something unusual were to arise he might have to review his charge although he would let the client know at the earliest opportunity.

15. For the charging of executries, Solicitors will in addition to the General Regulations require to refer to Chapter 5 of the Table of Fees. Commissions remain as previously but Solicitors will require to charge either detailed charges or alternatively according to circumstances. For the calculable elements comprising letters, telephone calls, meetings (including travelling time), perusal and drafting of documents, etc, or for time expended, consideration would have to be given as to whether any appropriate weighting or supplementary factor should be applied, such as in respect of the amount or value of any money or property involved.

Factors in charging according to circumstances

These are the factors referred to in General Regulation 4 and the following comments may be of assistance.

(a) The importance of the matter to the client

Most clients consider their own matters to be important, but apart from emotional importance to the client, this factor covers gains achieved or losses averted through the efforts of the practitioner, eg, the value of advice that heals a family rift, facilitates a reconciliation, settles a dispute amicably, or effects continuing tax savings, may be hard to quantify but should be considered under this factor. Both objective and subjective importance are relevant. It may be necessary to consider reducing the fee where the client has not recognised the matter as important to him.

A client is unlikely to wish a practitioner to devote considerable time and effort to a matter which the client regards as being of minor importance. Where a practitioner does so without the prior understanding and approval of the client, he is likely to find it necessary to apply a negative weighting factor to arrive at a fee which the client will find fair and reasonable. Client communication can be vital in this area.

While most clients will generally recognise the relevance of very satisfactory results achieved as a positive factor in the fixing of a fee, on the other hand diligence and time-consuming application by the practitioner may nevertheless achieve a result which is unsatisfactory for the client. The Solicitor will require to assess objectively whether this is due to the inherent factors of the case or whether the Solicitor himself has failed to concentrate his time and skill on those aspects of the transaction which are most critical or has failed to take advantage of an aspect which might have benefited the client. If the end result has been adversely affected some negative weighting may be called for.

(b) The amount or value of any money or property involved

This will be an ingredient in most conveyancing and executry transactions and many practitioners may experience difficulty in determining the weight to be ascribed to this factor in particular transactions until they gain experience in charging according to circumstances. Practice units may require to develop their own internal guidelines for determining the weight to be given to this factor in certain types of transaction, eg, domestic sales and purchase. It must be remembered that this factor, like all others, must be subservient to the overall test of a fair and reasonable charge and practitioners must be careful to assess the value element of the charge in each case on its merits using any percentage, bands of value, or other approach is a guide and no more. See also General Regulation 5(c) and paragraph 5 of the guidelines.

(c) The complexity of the matter or the difficulty or novelty of the question raised

If a matter is particularly difficult or involves some novel questions, it will normally receive positive weighting. The necessity to move into little known areas, particularly where little assistance can be obtained, is of considerable relevance. Unusually complex questions or particularly complicated assets involved may well justify an increased charge. It would, however, be necessary for the matter to involve greater complexity, difficulty or novelty than is usual for a fee earner of the particular hourly rate in order to justify positive weighting. It must, however, be carefully weighed, in particular also with (e) below (time expended), in order to justify a charge by an inexperienced practitioner spending excessive time in doing work beyond his normal competence. Conversely, if a practitioner with a high hourly charge rate chooses to handle a particularly straightforward matter (eg, the administration of a simple estate) this factor may produce negative weighting.

(d) The skill, labour, specialised knowledge and responsibility involved on the part of the solicitor or assistant

Special expertise or particular skill are relevant positive factors in fee charging. The responsibility element could include negotiations entrusted to the practitioner or acting for a client who relies on the practitioner to make an important decision on the client's behalf. The degree to which this factor should apply in fixing a fee must depend to a considerable extent on the basic hourly rate charged by the practitioner. If his hourly rate is high then the time and labour element itself will incorporate a reasonable degree of skill, special knowledge and responsibility.

(e) The time expended

This is the one ingredient common to all transactions and has already been discussed (see paragraphs 6–8). Where a fee earner has an hourly rate in keeping with his level of skill and experience and is engaged in work appropriate for such level of skill and experience in certain areas of work, the time and labour factor may of itself produce an appropriate charge without any weighting (either positive or negative) under the other factors.

(f) The length, number and importance of any documents or other papers prepared or perused

The length and number of documents may well overlap with factor (c) (complexity) and 'importance' in this context may well overlap with 'importance' discussed under factor (a) above (importance to the client). The preparation of a document requiring much original thought and/or specialised drafting could produce a significant positive weighting factor. Preparing or perusing a large number of documents associated with a transaction may justify an extra charge because of the need to consider their inter-relationship. In many cases the length and number of documents will be amply reflected in the time taken without the need for any allowance under this factor.

(g) The place where and the circumstances in which the services or any part thereof are rendered, including the degree of expedition required

The necessity to be away from the office or unavailable to other clients could increase overheads and justify an additional charge. Urgency can involve several aspects. Stress, postponing or delegating other work, intrusion into family or leisure time are obvious examples. Overtime made necessary by the urgency of the client's business is a justifiable reason for an increased charge. Overtime made necessary because the Solicitor has taken on more than he can cope with in his normal time is not such a reason. Nevertheless, urgency may mean that not only must the practitioner work quickly but possibly there may be little margin for error and no time available for careful review. Special expedition rendered necessary by the nature of the transaction or in response to the client's particular request is an important part of the circumstances in which the business is transacted and can justify increased remuneration.

If, on the other hand, there has been delay in carrying out the work, that might call for a reduction under this factor.

Most clients, particularly those in the commercial area, regard the effort and urgency accorded as relevant factors in the feeing process. However, much legal work of its very nature has some urgent aspects, for example, a conveyancing transaction proceeding to a settlement. Unless the nature or circumstances of the transaction or the requirements of the client demand expedition outside the ordinary, weighting under this factor would not normally be appropriate.

Simple guide to the Solicitors (Scotland) Accounts Rules 1995*

This booklet is issued as a guide and is *not* a substitute for the Rules and Regulations of which all solicitors should have a thorough knowledge.

SOME QUESTIONS AND ANSWERS

1. What is the main purpose of the rules?

To protect clients' money and to ensure that at all times solicitors identify and record client funds so that they may be clearly identified from the solicitor's own monies and to ensure that at all times solicitors have enough money in their client bank accounts to meet the total amount that they are due to clients (irrespective of any money due to them by clients) both as a solicitor and as a trustee in the course of their practice.

2. What is a client account?

It is any account with any bank or building society in the name of the solicitor but specifically identified in its title as being for clients or for a named client or trust etc. You can have as many client accounts as you need. The client account may also be a loan (but not a general deposit) to a local authority but in this case it must be in the name of the solicitor for a specific client. In the case of a *joint deposit* this should be recorded in the name of the first firm named and recorded as clients' funds by them.

3. Can the client account be with any bank or building society?

No. It must be with an authorised institution within the meaning of the Banking Act 1987, Clause 2(1) of the Accounts Rules or the Bank of England, National Savings Bank and the Post Office. It may also be an authorised building society under the Building Societies Act 1986. Any such institution must be able to operate within the banker's automated clearing system, details of 'recognised' institutions can be obtained from the Society or the Bank of England. If you deposit the clients' money with an institution that does not come within the definition of a client account then you must have the client's written consent.

4. What books must we keep and can they be electronic?

You must keep a cash book and a ledger in which there must be an account for every client in respect of whom you have any financial intromissions.

The Rules also require a separate record to be kept for inter-client transfers within the client ledgers (you must also keep a record of all other financial dealings of the firm and all accounting information must be up to date. The narrative for the entries needs to be clear and each entry should be self explanatory). If the books are on a computer it must have software to allow the accounting information to be printed out on request. Alternatively, books can be handwritten. This must be in ink and not in pencil.

5. Should we have a surplus or float in our general clients' bank account?

Yes. Most firms do as a simple precaution to cover minor mistakes which may occur from time-to-time. The reconciliations have to be listed and the statements kept for at least 18 months.

6. Do we need a compliance partner?

Yes. He or she is responsible for compliance with the Accounts Rules.

7. What do we do with money coming into the firm?

Immediately clients' money comes into the office, ensure that appropriate entries are made in the cash book; *do it today and not tomorrow!* Clients' money must be lodged in a properly designated bank account – it must not go through the office bank account.

8. What do we do about money going out?

Firstly ensure that you have funds to make the payment, normally by cheque. If you do not have sufficient client funds from the client account then you must use the firm's funds to meet any shortfall. If clients' funds are on SSD (solicitors special deposit account) or similar they must be uplifted and paid into the bank account on which the cheque is to be written before you issue the cheque or make payment from that account.

9. Why must we record entries for funds not paid through the client bank account?

The Rules now emphasise the need to record entries which are needed for completeness and to ensure that the client accounting records deal with the whole consideration involved in conveyancing transactions. Some elements of the price of property are paid to the solicitor in the form of a cheque made out to a third party. These cheques should now be recorded on the face of the ledger card as a contra entry.

10. How do we deal with bridging loans?

Do not enter into a bridging loan agreement on behalf of the client in circumstances which may impose on you personal liability for repayment in the event of default by the client. Bridging loans must always be in writing with full details of the client and what the arrangements are for repayment.

11. Can we lend money to a client?

Yes, but you are *not* protected by the Guarantee Fund.

12. Can we borrow money from a client?

No, unless the client has been independently advised about the loan or is in the business of lending money.

(NB. Loans from members of your family may not be covered by the Guarantee Fund.)

13. Do we need to keep a list of powers of attorney?

Yes, each year the compliance partners must do a complete list which includes both active and dormant powers of attorney in the name of any partner.

14. What records do we have to keep to operate a power of attorney?

A clear record of money paid in or out of the client's own bank account should be kept in a client ledger and cash book. Where you have exclusive control of the client's bank account then that bank balance should be treated as client funds which should be included in invested funds held for named clients.

15. What do we have to do on a daily basis?

For a manual system ensure that the cash book entries are also entered in the client's or the firm's ledger. The cash book and the ledger should be summed up to date and regularly balanced. They should clearly identify monies which you hold in separate client accounts.

A computer system will do this automatically provided you enter the information accurately and daily.

16. What are other funds?

These are funds which you hold in individual client accounts in the firm's name or in a solicitor's name in trust for a client. These include funds held under powers of attorney. Keep an extra column or section in your cash book or day book to record these. There must also be an additional column in the client's individual record headed 'Other Funds' or you could have a separate ledger card dealing with investment funds only. You are required to keep this separate record and to *reconcile* (physically check the balances in the account against the records) at least four times a year (many firms do this monthly).

17. What do we have to do to reconcile?

You check that all interest earned on building society or SSD accounts has been written up in the pass book or bank statements and that there is an equivalent entry on the face of the client records. You then prepare a list of investment funds and check this against the total of funds held in the investment account for the various authorised bodies. Any differences between the figures must be identified and adjusted to the correct amount. You must also keep the reconciliation lists for at least 18 months.

18. What do we have to do about interest on a client account – can we keep it?

In certain circumstances, yes. As a general rule when you have received money from a client you should put it into some form of interest bearing account for that client. This, however, depends upon the amount of money being lodged and/or the time it is likely to be held. You must always act fairly and reasonably. Smaller sums (under £500) which should be paid out within two months do not require to earn interest for the client. However larger sums, even for short periods, do. Particular attention should be paid to executry funds. Make sure that they too earn interest for the client.

19. Money laundering regulations – do they affect us?

Yes. This is not an easy subject and you will need to read the regulations at the end of this booklet.

(a) To whom do they apply?

Everybody.

(b) To what do the provisions apply?

- to every one-off transaction which involves the payment by or to the client of an amount of ECU 15,000 (approximately £12,000) or more, and to any one-off transaction for a smaller amount which appears to be linked with others where the aggregate of the amounts involved is in excess of ECU 15,000,
- to every case where the firm forms or resolves to form a business relationship for relevant financial business only,
- if you suspect that your client is engaged in money laundering, or that a transaction is being carried out on behalf of someone else who is engaged in money laundering.

The definitions of 'relevant financial business', 'business relationship' and 'one-off transactions' are set out at the end of this guide. The definitions are wide and any transaction which involves the handling of money of ECU 15,000 (approximately £12,000) or more, is likely to be subject to the money laundering provisions.

(c) What does this mean in practice?

Some matters are *exempt*. Examples are:
- Existing clients do not require identification checks
- Instructions from other agents who confirm to you that they have complied (reg 10)
- Cheques drawn on the clients own UK bank account (reg 8)

– Criminal work, wills, licensing and gaming work, insurance claims, certain matrimonial matters etc.

(d) Can you give us one or two practical examples?

Matters which are unlikely to be exempt and therefore covered would be:
House purchase (unless all funds from client's own UK bank account)
Investment of client's funds
Receipt of funds for onwards transmission to the client or a third party.

(e) When did these new Regulations come into effect?

The Money Laundering Regulations 1993 (the 'Regulations') came into force on 1 April 1994 for relevant financial business.

(f) When did our rules on money laundering come into effect?

The Society's Rules came into force on 1 May 1994.

(g) What are the Regulations supposed to do?

Prevent the proceeds of unlawful activities being legitimised by being applied to carry out legitimate transactions.

(h) What do we have to do under the Regulations?

1. verify the identity of every person with whom you intend to form a business relationship, or carry out a one-off transaction;
2. maintain record keeping procedures; and
3. maintain internal reporting procedures.

(i) What happens if we do not comply?

Failure to comply with the Regulations constitutes a criminal offence, punishable by a fine and/or imprisonment for a term of up to 2 years!

(j) What else do we have to do?

Set up and maintain a procedure for establishing the identity of a client where required in terms of the rules and regulations (see (b) above).

(k) Do we have to identify clients?

Yes. If satisfactory evidence of the identity of new clients is not obtained then the business relationship or one-off transaction as the case may be shall not proceed any further.

(l) How do we go about deciding if we need to comply and also in identifying new clients?

Common sense. However if in doubt there is a style of Verification of Identity Flowchart annexed at Schedule 1 and an Evidence of Identity form at Schedule 2.

(m) When is evidence of identity satisfactory?

1. when it is reasonably capable of establishing that the applicant is the person he claims to be and
2. when the person who obtains the evidence is satisfied, in accordance with the procedures maintained under the Regulations, that the evidence does establish that the applicant is the person he claims to be.

For **individual clients** it is suggested you obtain:
- the true name and/or names used
- current permanent address, including postcode
- 'wherever possible' the date and place of birth
- a document from a reputable source which has a photograph of the applicant eg a current valid full passport or national identity card should be requested and the number recorded.

other suggestions:
- check the voters' roll
- make a credit reference agency search
- see an original recent electricity, gas, telephone, council tax bill or bank statement
- check a local telephone directory
- visit their home

For **corporate clients**
No specific steps are needed if clients are:
- a listed company or a subsidiary of a listed company
- a private company or partnership one or more of whose directors/partners are already known to the firm.

Steps are needed if clients are:
an unquoted company or a partnership and none of the directors/partners is already known, then the firm should verify the identity of one or more of the principal directors/partners and/or shareholders as applicable as if they were individual clients, see above.

It is suggested you also obtain copies of:
Certificate of incorporation/certificate of trade or equivalent and perhaps for companies their latest report and accounts (audited where applicable).

(n) What records do we have to keep and for how long?

The evidence of identity you obtained needs to be kept for at least 5 years from completion of the relevant business or transaction concerned.

(o) Do we have to have a money laundering reporting officer?

Yes.

(p) What do we have to tell him/her?

Any information or other matter which comes to the attention of a person handling relevant financial business which in the opinion of the person hand-ling that business gives rise to a knowledge or suspicion of money laundering.

(q) What does the money laundering reporting officer have to do?

Consider all such reports and any other relevant information and decide if this gives rise to a knowledge or suspicion of money laundering. If so pass that information to NCIS.

(r) How?

Use the style of form in Schedule 3.
In serious cases telephone or fax NCIS to get guidance on how to proceed with a suspicious transaction.

Telephone Number: 0171 238 8274
Fax Number: 0171 238 8286

(s) What else should they do?

Keep a record of what they decide to do and why.

20. We only do legal aid work, do we need to keep clients' accounts?

It is common practice for cheques paid by The Scottish Legal Aid Board to be paid directly into the firm's bank account or another special bank account set up for this purpose. Many firms do not have a client bank account for this. However, it is important to note that when SLAB's cheque or telegraphic transfer is paid into the firm's bank account it is essential that you have already paid out the outlays due to third parties and these funds are simply reimbursements. If some, or all of the outlays have not been settled then that portion of SLAB's remittance in this respect is clients' funds and should be treated as such. However, settle-ment of such outlays on the date of receipt is acceptable. If you are not able to do that then you must have a client bank account or you will be in breach of the bank's rules.

21. Inter-client loans – are they protected by the Guarantee Fund?

Normally not. Make sure the lending client gives written consent to the loan and written confirmation that they understand that they will have no claim on the Guarantee Fund. Consider very carefully the question of conflict of interest in any such transaction. Remember the conflict rule No. 10!

22. When can we take fees?

After you have rendered a fee note and if you have funds in the client account. Do not draw fees when you do not have a balance to meet them as this is likely to result in a deficit in the client bank account and lead you to being in breach of the Rules. Take care to ensure that interim fees are fair and reasonable and reflect the work which has already been done.

23. Do I have to balance the firm's books?

Yes. You must keep all your accounting records up to date at all times and balance your books monthly. That is all your books, your client's account, your own funds and your assets and liabilities. The obligation is to have them balanced throughout the practice year and your accountant, in the accountant's certificate, requires to certify that this has been done. You must also properly maintain your own firm's records so the true financial position of the practice can be ascertained at all times. If in any doubt of this aspect of the rules contact your own accountant or the accountants' department of the Law Society (see below).

24. What is an accountant's certificate?

The annual certificate produced by your accountant under the Accountant's Certificate Rules has to be produced annually and within six months of the end of your year. Please ensure that you diary a reminder and your accountants have the certificate prepared for lodging in good time. *Do not leave it until the last minute!* You do not have to have a complete audit of the whole books of the firm but the preparation of the accountant's certificate for the firm's trial balance at the accounting period is normally sufficient to allow the certificate to be completed. Applications for extensions beyond the six month deadline are rarely granted.

Note:

This brief guide has been prepared by the Guarantee Fund Committee who are solicitors just like yourselves. None of us likes rules but they are there to help us all keep proper records, to protect clients' money, to reduce the risk to the Guarantee Fund and to keep the Guarantee Fund contributions to a minimum.

Please play your part

If you are at any time in doubt about what you are doing, please do not hesitate to contact the Society's Chief Accountant Leslie Cumming or one of his staff at:

The Law Society of Scotland
The Law Society's Hall
26 Drumsheugh Gardens
Edinburgh
EH3 7YR

(Document Exchange DX ED1 EDINBURGH)

Telephone: 0131 226 7411
Fax: 0131 225 2934

who are always willing to help and advise.

SUPPLEMENTARY GUIDANCE ON COMMON PROBLEMS ON THE ACCOUNTS RULES

Recent inspections carried out by the Guarantee Fund monitoring team have identified a surprisingly large number of solicitors who have not revised the accounting systems to ensure compliance with the 1992 Rules. This is resulting in an extra workload being placed on the inspectors and is delaying the reduction in the monitoring cycle time which is targeted for a two year cycle.

The routine reports show a lack of appreciation of the need to introduce new systems in three main areas:

(a) Rule 6(3) – client cheque designation

Including the client name or account number on all cheques payable to banks or building societies is an obligation imposed on solicitors in September 1992. Many honest solicitors have still failed to make this simple change. This is adding to the investigation work and is having to be reported to the Committee. This change was introduced because of the easy solution which it gave to dishonest solicitors or employees who want to divert funds from their legitimate designation. The administrative problems of vouching such payments means that a fraudster can continue to divert funds amongst a large number of honest disbursements which are not being specifically designated as required by the Rule. It is a simple step which should not be delayed any longer.

(b) Rule 12(3) (a) (ii) – the inter-client ledger transfers

The Rules require solicitors to keep a separate journal record of any transfer entries between client ledgers. This did not include transfers between separate matters records held for the same client but did include:

(i)   Transfer of sale/purchase price between two clients within the client ledger.
(ii) Loans between clients.
(iii) Posting corrections of an operator error or coding error which have to go through the client accounts. All of these types of entries have been misused by fraudsters who are manoeuvring funds within the client accounts either to cover an earlier fraud or to position money into a ledger card which can be operated without suspicion.

(c) Rule 14 – reconciliation of funds held invested on behalf of named clients

Again the Rules require a quarterly check to be carried out on the substantial funds held by legal firms in separate named accounts. Evidence that the working reconciliations are completed has been destroyed or are not available. Errors in this area of accounting are found which indicate that solicitors are not checking properly that errors and omissions are being corrected.

(d) Clients' funds outwith the UK

The Guarantee Fund Committee has recently had occasion to address the question of client funds placed in bank accounts in the Channel Islands and the Isle of Man. Substantial sums of money are held in such locations in accounts which are set up by Scottish solicitors as required by the definition of client accounts contained in rule 2 of the Solicitors (Scotland) Accounts Rules 1995.

The accounts have generally been placed with a wholly owned subsidiary of an authorised financial institution and the account name contains both the solicitor's and the client's name.

Following an exchange of correspondence on such accounts the Guarantee Fund Committee is satisfied that such accounts *do not* comply with the terms of the definition under rule 2. The accounts need to be with a branch of the organisation *within the UK*. The Committee is satisfied that the Channel Islands and the Isle of Man are not part of the United Kingdom. Separate legal and banking jurisdictions apply to these territories.

Client account funds may only be invested in accounts outwith the UK with the express consent of the clients and suitable risk warnings must be given to the clients in advance of any decision to place funds in accounts which are outwith the scope of the Accounts Rules.

(e) Legal aid/legal advice and assistance

During a recent review of the Solicitors (Scotland) Accounts Rules 1992 and the Solicitors (Scotland) Accounts (Amendment) Rules 1994 a working party consisting of Guarantee Fund members and seconded members in practice were invited to consider a number of issues which might require rules to be amended or extended.

One of the matters considered was *the accounting treatment of legal aid contributions from clients and the receipt of outlays paid by the Scottish Legal Aid Board.* Those entries are specifically referred to in other Accounts Rules as applied in other jurisdictions in the UK. The working party agreed that the current set of Accounts Rules clearly covered these points but these were not being interpreted in the correct manner either by the profession or the Guarantee Fund inspection team.

This guidance will remind the profession on two matters:
 (i) Contributions received from clients who are in receipt of legal aid or legal advice and assistance *must* be treated as client funds until an account is rendered as required by rule 6(1)(*d*).
 (ii) Outlays incurred on behalf of legal aid clients *must* be properly dealt with in the accounts ledger. Any outlays which have not been paid out by the solicitor at the date of settlement by the Legal Aid Board amount to funds received on behalf of clients and must be passed into the client bank account until funds are disbursed to the third party involved.

Contributions and outlays in (*a*) and (*b*) above can be excluded from the client account only if the account is raised and rendered and all outlays are disbursed before the funds are received from the Scottish Legal Aid Board. The working party agreed that payments made on the same day of receipt from the Legal Aid Board would comply with the demands of the Rules.

Unless the payments are made at the correct date the solicitor will need to set up client accounting systems. This will *not* affect the master policy discounts available to specialist practitioners.

Members and their cashroom staff should ensure that their own arrangements comply fully with this advice since *failure* to address these issues *may result* in solicitors being in breach of the Solicitors (Scotland) Accounts Rules 1995 rules 4(1) and 7(a) and (f).

SUGGESTED LIST OF ITEMS THAT SHOULD BE SPECIAL AREAS OF CONCERN TO DESIGNATED CASH ROOM PARTNERS

Consider:

1. The methods used to record incoming funds and make sure that all funds are lodged in the bank on the day of receipt.

2. Your arrangements to handle cash handed in by clients.
   eg Do you have special arrangements to cope with larger cash sums brought to you by clients?

Do you see the detailed workings of the client account balances each month?

How much checking do you do each month on:

a. Lists of client balances
b. Bank reconciliation working papers
c. Statements of surplus / deficit

Do you have an automatic reporting and investigation procedure set up if your accounting system discloses a temporary shortage?

Can you confirm at least quarterly that all client funds including funds invested for named clients are properly accounted for? What checks are done to verify the position?

Are all large fees reviewed to confirm they are fully charged but not excessively or prematurely charged?

Do you have any controls over the level of interim fees being charged during an ongoing piece of business?

GUIDANCE ON RETENTION / DESTRUCTION OF FILES AND RECORDS

Specific obligations regarding the retention of financial records are noted in the Solicitors (Scotland) Accounts Rules. The client ledger records and day book records or journals must be retained for a period of ten years. The Law Society therefore recommends that any documents which may be required to be produced to vouch payments or receipts within the client ledger account should also be retained for a period of ten years.

Client files which deal with conveyancing, executry or trust accounting matters would contain within the general correspondence files matters of importance which would require to be kept for the full ten-year period. Bank statements, cashed cheques, VAT fee notes or any passbooks or print-outs which relate to funds invested or borrowed on behalf of clients would fall directly into this category.

Those solicitors who use a system of debit / credit posting slips to instruct the cashroom in their work should also ensure that these documents are retained safely for the ten-year period. Previous advice from the Society had suggested that these posting slips might not require to be retained for the full ten-year period. Police enquiries into matters of employee or solicitor fraud have now indicated that these documents are of vital significance to their enquiry since the handwriting will give significant evidence as regards the source of instructions in respect of any misleading or false entries. You may wish to take account of this advice.

The only financial records which are not covered by the ten-year rule are the documents which comprise lists of client balances, bank reconciliation workings and statement of surplus / deficit prepared in respect of the monthly client ledger account reconciliation. These working papers are only required to be kept for a period of eighteen months.

The Society is aware that a convention has grown up amongst solicitors who carry out a significant amount of criminal legal aid whereby files which relate to completed cases are routinely destroyed twelve months after the matter has been concluded. The Society has no concerns regarding this procedure provided there are no client account funds involved in the transaction. In the event that the solicitor is dealing with client funds any relevant vouchers would require to be separated and stored for the full ten-year period prior to the contents of the file being destroyed.

Generally if you are in doubt with regard to the destruction of specific client files or papers then every effort should be made to retain all documents for the minimum ten years.

Handbook to the Investment Business Rules and Regulations*

CONTENTS

* © The Law Society of Scotland, November 1994

Client fact sheet
  (i)   Executry
 (ii)   Trust
(iii)   Power of attorney
(iv)   Curatory

Part IV – Life Assurance and Unit Trusts

Packaged products
  (i)   Client refuses to give some details
 (ii)   Client gives you incorrect or misleading information
(iii)   Clients ask you to complete the client fact sheet

Unit trusts

Pensions business – transfer or opt-out from an occupational pension scheme

Part V – Management and Compliance

Management letter
  (i)   Part A – Positive return
        Section 1 – Extent of investment business
        Section 2 – Scope of investment business
        Section 3 – Scale of securities transactions and investment management
        Section 4 – Life policies and units in collective investment schemes
        Section 5 – Investment Business Training Regulations
        Section 6 – Compliance
 (ii)   Part B – Nil return
(iii)   Compliance certificate

Part VI – Discipline

Complaints from the Public
Other Powers

PART I – INTRODUCTION

Regulatory structure

The financial services industry within the United Kingdom is governed by the Financial Services Act 1986 (FSA) which became fully operational in April 1988. The purpose of the Act is to regulate all investment advisers and to provide protection for investors. The Act provides a structure for all those who wish to conduct investment business.

The Securities and Investments Board (SIB) is ultimately responsible for the regulatory environment although it has delegated the day-to-day management of investment business to a number of other organisations which can broadly be divided into two groups as follows:

(1) Self regulating organisations (SRO)

From the middle of 1995 there will only be three SROs who will be (a) Securities and Futures Authority (SFA) – regulates firms which deal in or advise on securities, futures and options; (b) Investment Management Regulatory Organisation (IMRO) – regulates firms whose main function is managing funds ie investment fund managers; and (c) Personal Investment Authority (PIA) – regulates life companies, unit trust companies and independent financial advisers.

(2) Recognised professional bodies (RPB)

There are currently nine RPBs who are responsible for regulating their own professional members who wish to conduct investment business.

The Law Society of Scotland has been an RPB since 1988 and it can therefore authorise firms who wish to conduct investment business. The Society is accordingly responsible to SIB for the conduct of its members under the FSA. The Society's detailed procedures on how firms must conduct investment business are contained in the undernoted rules:

(1) Solicitors (Scotland) Investment Business Training Regulations 1994;
(2) Solicitors (Scotland) (Conduct of Investment Business) Practice Rules 1994;
(3) Solicitors (Scotland) Compliance Certificate Rules 1994;
– all of which came into operation on 1 July 1994, and
(4) Solicitors (Scotland) (Conduct of Investment Business) (Amendment) Practice Rules 1994 – effective from 1 January 1995.

There is also a 'Simple Guide' issued for the first three sets of rules and a separate guide for the Amendment Rules.

A firm which wishes to conduct investment business has to apply to the Society which on approval of the firm's application issues an Investment Business Certificate (IBC) to the applicant. This certificate must be displayed in the firm's premises.

The IBC authorises a firm to conduct all manner of investment business apart from the five prohibited areas listed in rule 3.2. It should also be noted that with effect from 1 July 1995 a firm can only give advice or make arrangements for clients in relation to transfers or opt-outs from occupational pension schemes if the firm has the specific prior approval of the Society.

A firm must pay an annual subscription to the Society to maintain its IBC. The fee for 1994/95 is made up of a flat fee of £129 plus a fee of £55 per partner (up to a ceiling of 15 partners). The maximum fee a firm will pay for its authorisation is therefore £954.

Investment Business Training Regulations

One of the major changes introduced by the Society in its investment business regime is the requirement for those individuals conducting investment business to have undertaken some form of investment business training. The new investment business training regime comes into force on 1 November 1995 and consists of an Investment Business Examination and a requirement to undertake Continuing Professional Development (CPD) in investment business.

The Investment Business Examination the Society is promoting is the Investment Advice Certificate (a three-paper examination) of the Securities Institute which is a professional financial training body based in London.

The Society has recognised as equivalent qualifications to the Securities Institute's Investment Advice Certificate the following examinations:

(1) The Financial Planning Certificate of the Chartered Insurance Institute;
(2) Membership of the Securities Institute;
(3) The Securities Institute Diploma; and
(4) The Associate Examination of the Institute of Investment Management and Research.

From 1 November 1995 the Society will only continue to authorise a firm to conduct investment business if there is at least *one partner* in the firm who is either:

(a) exempt from the Society's examination; or
(b) has passed the Society's examination; or
(c) holds an investment qualification (as above) equivalent to the Society's examination.

All other solicitors and non-solicitors conducting investment business within an authorised firm must be qualified in terms of (a), (b) or (c) above.

An exemption procedure was set up under the Investment Business Training Regulations so that those individuals experienced in investment business could apply for exemption from the requirement to sit the Investment Business Examination. The exemption forms were sent out to authorised firms in August 1994. The deadline for submission of an exemption application form to the Society was 30 November 1994.

A solicitor could apply for an exemption if:

(a) he has held a full and unrestricted practising certificate for a continuous period of not less than 5 years ending on 31 October 1994; and
(b) he has had sufficient investment business experience in the 3 years prior to 31 October 1994.

A non-solicitor could also have applied for an exemption if he satisfied condition (b) above and had been in continuous employment in investment business for not less than 3 years ending on 31 October 1994.

The fee for an exemption was £20 per applicant.

If an individual did not get an exemption or is a new intrant to the profession there are only two options open to such a person if they wish to conduct investment business – these being either pass the Investment Advice Certificate or one of its equivalent examinations.

The CPD requirement is that from 1 November 1995 all individuals conducting investment business must undertake 5 hours of investment business CPD per annum. The CPD can be either private or group study and a record of compliance must be maintained.

Types of investments and investment business

The definition of an investment is given in FSA, Schedule 1 Part 1. Bank and building society deposits, most national savings products and term assurance policies (eg mortgage protection policies) are not investments for the purposes of the Act. The FSA lists five different types of activity which constitute investment business, these are:

(1) dealing in investments on behalf of others;
(2) arranging deals in investments;
(3) managing investments;
(4) advising on investments;
(5) establishing or operating a collective investment scheme (unit trusts).

It is FSA, Schedule 2 Parts 2 and 3 which list the activities constituting investment business.

Involvement of solicitors in investment business

The types of investment products solicitors will mostly deal with are (a) shares; (b) government (GILTs) and local authority stocks; (c) life assurance policies (eg an endowment); (d) pension policies.

There are four levels of involvement which a firm may have in conducting investment business and these are:

(1) **Execution only** – this is where a firm effects a transaction for a client and where the client does not rely on the firm to advise him on or to exercise any judgment on his behalf as to the merits or the suitability for him of the transaction (eg the client comes in and gives a clear instruction to the solicitor to buy 10,000 ICI shares).

(2) **Taking instructions but giving no advice** – here the client wishes to make some investments and the solicitor merely obtains the advice of a specialist financial adviser (ie a stockbroker) and then communicates the specialist's advice to the client but giving no comment on the specialist's advice. This activity does not fall within the definition of 'portfolio management'.

(3) **Taking instructions but giving advice** – here the client seeks the solicitor's views on what investments he should make. The solicitor again obtains advice from a specialist financial services adviser but this time the solicitor comments on the advice of the specialist.

(4) **Investment management** – there are two types of investment management which a firm may enter into:

    (a) *Portfolio management* – here the firm has assumed responsibility for advising or commenting upon the investments comprised in a client's portfolio; or

    (b) *Discretionary portfolio management* – as (a) above but the firm has authority to effect transactions for the portfolio at its discretion.

Most portfolios are made up of shares and/or GILTs but it is possible for a portfolio to include Unit Trusts. In the case of a discretionary portfolio the Council of the Society may require the Discretionary Portfolio Manager to lodge a Bond of Caution with the Society (see rule 10.1).

There are two basic principles which underline the conduct of all investment business and these are:

(1) **Best advice (rule 4.4)** – to give a client 'best advice' a firm must (a) 'know the client' and (b) 'know the market'.

In order for a firm to know a client, a client factsheet must be prepared for that client in advance of conducting investment business. The client must also be informed of the nature of the risks involved in any investment transaction.

A firm to show that it 'knows the market' in relation to:

(a) shares – must obtain regular updates from stockbrokers and read the relevant national newspapers and financial magazines etc.

(b) insurance products – must keep abreast of the insurance company tables and read the national newspapers and financial magazines.

Best advice is then a combination of 'knowing the client' and 'knowing the market'. The net result of this process will be that a firm should be able to make a recommendation on a particular product which is most suitable to a particular client in order to ensure that client's investment objectives are met.

(2) **Best execution (rule 4.5)** – once a firm 'knows its client' and 'knows the market' and has therefore given best advice the next step is to acquire or sell the product for the client in line with the rule on best execution which means effecting or arranging the investment transaction with due timeliness and on terms that may reasonably be regarded as the best available at the time in the interests of the client.

Terms of business

Client terms of business (rule 4.6) – a statement of terms of business must be provided to a client where a firm undertakes non-discretionary portfolio management. The terms of business must comply with the relevant parts of Schedule 1(1). The terms of business statement can be in the form of a letter which need only be sent to the client.

It is only where a firm is undertaking discretionary portfolio management that the terms of business statement must be in the form of a written contract complying with the terms of Schedule 1(2) and which must be signed and returned by clients. Furthermore where a firm has established itself as a plan manager of its own personal equity plan, terms of business must also be entered into in terms of Schedule 1. It should be noted that existing client agreements will continue to have effect.

Rule 4.7 requires a firm to retain a copy of all statements of terms of business and written contracts entered into for both forms of portfolio management and PEP management and client agreements entered into under the old Investment Business Practice Rules 1989. The copies must be kept for 10 years from the time when the terms of business or written contract provided cease to be effective.

PART II – STOCKS AND SHARES

Introduction

The Society's record keeping requirements are contained in Part 6 of the Investment Business Practice Rules. Good record keeping is essential as it ensures that there is an audit trail for the Society's inspecting accountants and a firm's own auditors to follow. Many of the record keeping requirements represent good business practice, examples of which are:
(1) All incoming mail must be date-stamped (even if it is dealt with on the day of receipt).
(2) All telephone calls must be recorded.
(3) All meetings must be recorded.
Date-stamping provides evidence of compliance with rule 4.5 on Best Execution to the effect that clients' instructions have been effected or arranged with due timeliness.

The basic record keeping requirements are contained in rule 6.1 and it should be noted that the transaction records required under this rule are common to both share transactions and life assurance and unit trust transactions.

Rule 6.1 requires that a firm keep records of:
(a) all instructions received from clients to effect investment transactions and all decisions to effect transactions which are taken on behalf of clients;
(b) all instructions given to other persons to effect investment transactions on behalf of clients; and
(c) all investment transactions which have been effected on behalf of clients (which for a stock exchange transaction, means keeping a copy of the relevant contract note).

The firm's record of compliance with these general obligations must be kept for ten years. There are also additional record keeping requirements which are specific to stock exchange investments and these are detailed below.

A firm has basically two options in terms of record keeping for stock exchange transactions. A firm can either maintain careful individual file records for each client in relation to their stock exchange transactions or alternatively maintain a daily record book.

(1) **Daily record book** – the daily record book is an 'audit trail' of all stock exchange transactions carried out by the firm. The firm's financial services compliance officer should have overall responsibility if a firm maintains a daily record book.

The daily record book (which of course can be computerised) will contain entries for all mail relating to stock exchange transactions and thereafter records of telephone calls, meetings etc. The daily record book is vouched by letters, records of telephone calls, records of meetings, contract notes, share certificates etc.

Where a daily record book is maintained this will also have to be backed-up with a central record of all client transactions, which will entail a record card for each client showing the various stock exchange transactions carried out on their behalf.

(2) **Individual client investment files** – under this system each client is provided with their own investment file which will contain the vouchers for each transaction on a client by client basis. Such individual client files could be opened for each investment year in order to prevent the files becoming unwieldy.

There are a number of other documents which are important in relation to Stock Exchange transactions and these are:

(1) **Client factsheet** – this is a simple question and answer form which shows that the firm 'knows the client' and that sufficient investigation has been undertaken into the client's financial affairs to recognise what stock exchange investments (if any) are most suitable for the client. The individual client investment file will contain the original client factsheet.

(2) **Terms of business** – a firm must retain a copy of all statements of terms of business entered into for non-discretionary portfolio management. Furthermore all written contracts entered into for discretionary portfolio management must be maintained in the client file. Existing client agreements entered into under the Investment Business Practice Rules 1989 will continue to have effect.

(3) **Contract notes (rule 6.2)** – rule 6.2 requires the firm to send a copy of the contract note to the client evidencing the purchase or sale of the stock exchange investments. A copy of the contract note and the letter sending it out to the client should be kept on the client's file. It should be noted that in terms of rule 3.3 the contract note should state that the transaction is to be effected on behalf of the client.

(4) **Stock transfer forms** – a stock transfer form requires to be sent to the client when a sale of shares is effected. This form is obtained from a stockbroker and requires to be signed by the client.

(5) **Share certificates** – the dates on which share certificates are sent out and received must be recorded. As a matter of course a certificate should always be checked to confirm the registration details are correct. It is worth remembering that share certificates are not issued with the contract note.

Where a firm is merely holding a client's share certificate(s) for safekeeping purposes it should be noted that this does not constitute investment business.

(6) **List of clients' title documents** – a firm must maintain an up-to-date and accurate record of all documents of title relating to stock exchange investments. The list should record where the documents of title are kept and who is the beneficial owner of each of the investments.

When a sale is effected the list should be amended and when a purchase is made it should be recorded on the current list and the list updated as soon as the share certificate is received.

(7) **Managed portfolios reports** – where a firm is acting as a non-discretionary portfolio manager the client must be sent at least once a year a report stating the value of the portfolio at the beginning and end of the period to which the report relates and the portfolio's composition at the end of the period. Furthermore where the firm is acting as a

discretionary portfolio manager the report must state the changes in the composition between the start and the end of the period to which the report relates.

(8) Agreements with stockbrokers – a firm must retain a copy of any agreements it enters into with stockbrokers to effect clients' stock exchange transactions. A firm must also at least once a year review its agreement with stockbrokers to ensure that the stockbrokers are providing a good service to the client. This may be done by reference to the stockbroker's fees, commission and research material.

ROLLING SETTLEMENT

With effect from 18 July 1994 the Stock Exchange introduced rolling settlement for all share transactions. The mechanics of rolling settlement is that the new period between a trade and settlement will be 10 working days ie T+10. Hence if a firm deals for a client on Monday then settlement of that transaction must be completed on the Monday two weeks later. The Stock Exchange intend to introduce 5-day rolling settlement sometime in 1995 and it is likely that even shorter settlement periods will be introduced before the end of the century.

One effect of rolling settlement is that firms may consider holding clients' shares in a nominee company. The nominee company can be that of the firm's or that of a third party (such as stockbrokers). If a third party's nominee company is used the firm must be satisfied that this third party is suitable to act as a custodian of clients' share certificates. Before any clients' shareholdings are put in a nominee account the client must agree in writing to such transfers. The client should also be advised of the two types of nominee account; the first type being a designated nominee where a shareholder is directly and separately identified and the second is the undesignated or pooled nominee where the client's shareholdings are pooled with others for whom the nominee company acts.

The Bank of England intend introducing by the end of the century a new system of paperless shareholding known as CREST. Under CREST a shareholder will have the option of either maintaining his paper share certificates or holding his shares by electronic form.

PART III – TRUSTS AND EXECUTRIES

Introduction

Where a firm is involved in non-discretionary or discretionary portfolio management involving trusts and executries, the following procedures apply:

(1) Executry

Unless a transfer or sale of *all* the holdings in the estate is intimated at the time of the initial interview, a client terms of business/written contract should be concluded between the *executors* and the firm.

If the eventual beneficiaries of the shares are either clients of the firm (or indeed become clients of the firm) or are the executors of the estate a separate client terms of business/written contract is required between the individual beneficiary and the firm.

(2) Trusts

In a trust a client terms of business/written contract is required between all the *trustees* and the firm. If one trustee has been nominated to receive contract notes etc, this fact should be incorporated into the client terms of business/written contract which is signed by *all* trustees.

If the liferentrix or other trust beneficiary is a client of the firm he/she may also wish to conclude a client terms of business/written contract with the firm but this will be for a personal portfolio not the trust assets because the beneficiary has no right of investment over the liferented trust estate which would normally be invested to provide a balance between income and capital.

If any of the trustees are clients of the firm in their own right and wish the firm to deal in stocks and shares for them as individuals they should conclude a separate terms of business/written contract.

(3) Power of attorney

The client terms of business/written contract is concluded between the *attorney* and the firm *even if the attorney is a partner in the firm.*

(4) Curatory

The client terms of business/written contract is concluded between the *curator* and the firm *even if the curator is a partner in the firm.*

Client fact sheet

(1) Executry

Not required as the will speaks for itself.

(2) Trust

Not required as the will or trust deed speaks for itself.

(3) Power of attorney

Required. The client fact sheet will be about the person who signed the power of attorney – not the attorney.

(4) Curatory

Required. The client fact sheet is for the *incapax* – not the curator.

PART IV – LIFE ASSURANCE AND UNIT TRUSTS

Packaged products

This section deals with the rules on packaged products. A packaged product means a life policy, pension, unit trust or investment trust savings scheme. As for Stock Exchange transactions, a client fact sheet must be compiled before advice is given on any packaged product. The client fact sheet is a summary of a client's financial position and objectives. The client fact sheet (see example E4) should list the client's personal details, income, expenses, assets, investments, liabilities, any life assurance, pension, health insurance, investment objectives and any additional information.

A number of situations can arise when a client fact sheet is being prepared:

(1) **Client refuses to give some details** – In this situation the firm must obtain the client's signed acknowledgment of the fact that he refused to provide all information and a detailed note of this should be maintained in the client's file. If as a result of this the firm is not able to give best advice the firm should decline to act for the client in this matter.

(2) **Client gives you incorrect or misleading information (either innocently or on purpose)** – This circumstance is acceptable provided the firm makes an accurate record of what information the client does disclose and the firm acts in good faith throughout.

(3) **Clients ask you to complete the client fact sheet** – This is acceptable but the client must read over the client fact sheet carefully checking that all details are correct before signing it.

The general rules on record keeping contained in rule 6.1 apply equally to packaged products as they do to Stock Exchange investments. However there are a number of additional record keeping requirements for life assurance and unit trust business. The first additional requirement is contained in rule 6.6 under which a firm must maintain a separate record of the number of life policies and transactions in regulated collective investment schemes (ie unit trusts) placed directly or indirectly with each life office and/or unit trust company – postings to this central record should be done on a daily basis. The central record in respect of each transaction will contain:

(a) the name and address of the client;
(b) date policy/transaction effected;
(c) the name of the life policy/unit trust operator;
(d) type of policy/unit trust.

A typical entry in the central record book would be as below:

Client Details	Date Policy Arranged/ Transaction Effected	Life Office/ Operator	Type of Policy/ Units
Mrs AB Smith (address)	4.4.95	Scottish Widows	Low Cost Endowment
Mr CD Jones (address)	15.4.95	Foreign & Colonial	Far Eastern Trusts (1,000 Units

There are a number of additional requirements upon a firm when it advises in relation to a life policy and these are as follows:

(1) Under rule 4.4(2) from 1 January 1995 a firm must ensure that whenever it recommends a life policy to a client that the client is provided with a written statement of the key features relating to the policy including the policy's prospective surrender value. This 'key features' statement will be provided by life companies. From 1 July 1995 life companies must issue 'key features' statements which are client specific, ie so that the statement relates to a particular policy for a named client. It is the responsibility of the firm to ensure that the client receives the key features statement. It should be noted that where a life company does not produce a key features statement the firm must produce this statement.

(2) Under rule 4.4(3) whenever a firm recommends to a client to –
   (i) take on a long-term commitment (ie life policy or pension) or
   (ii) relinquish such a long-term commitment;
the firm must explain to the client *in writing* the reasons why the firm believes the commitment (or relinquishment) to be suitable. A firm must retain a copy of the 'reason why letter' in the client's file for a period of 3 years from the date on which the recommendation was given.

(3) Under rule 4.10 in respect of any life policy recommended, a firm must disclose to a client the commission that will be received on the sale of the life policy. The disclosure must be made in writing to the client and give the value of the commission in cash terms.
The typical paperwork to back up a life policy will therefore consist of:
   (a) Copy client fact sheet;
   (b) Copies of the quotations obtained;
   (c) The quotation selected should be marked with the reasons for its selection;
   (d) Copy of the 'reason why letter';
   (e) Copy of the 'key features' statement from the life company;
   (f) Copy of the completed (and dated) proposal form;
   (g) Copy of the covering letter sending the proposal form to the life company;
   (h) Copy reply from the life company detailing cover arranged; and
   (i) Appropriate record made in the central record (rule 6.6).

Unit trusts

The typical paperwork in a client's file relating to the purchase and/or sale of unit trusts will be as follows:

(1) Copy client fact sheet.
(2) Copies of the quotations obtained from a number of unit trust companies.
(3) Report on these quotations together with the recommendation for the client.
(4) Record recording the effecting of the purchase of the required unit trust for the client. Recording in the central record (rule 6.6) when the

transaction effected, name and address of the client, name and type of units bought and from which company.

(5) Copy letter sending contract note for unit trusts to client and letter containing cheque from client for sum due.

(6) Copy letter to unit trust company settling the purchase and / or sale.

Where a recommendation is made in relation to a unit trust the firm must disclose to the client that it will receive commission from the unit trust company and that details of such commission will be forthcoming from the company provided always that the firm will disclose to a client the amount of commission payable in respect of such transactions if the client so asks.

A number of firms when advising clients on packaged products merely refer them to another independent financial adviser who specialises in this area. Where a firm does make such a referral the requirements of best advice, knowing the client and knowing the market, then fall upon the other independent financial adviser.

It should be noted in this context that there are two different categories of adviser:

(1) Independent financial adviser – can recommend the products from any company;

(2) Company representative – recommends products from only one company.

Pensions business – transfer or opt-out from an occupational pension scheme

From 1 July 1995 any firm which wishes to give advice or make arrangements for clients in relation to a transfer or opt-out from an occupational pension scheme must obtain the specific prior approval of the Society to give such advice or make such arrangements.

With regard to an opt-out from an occupational pension scheme it is SIB's opinion that

'An Opt-Out is presumed to be adverse to the interests of the individual investor concerned unless the contrary can be affirmatively shown.'

It should be noted that this new regime of pension business does not relate to the giving of advice or the making of arrangements in relation to personal pensions.

PART V – MANAGEMENT & COMPLIANCE

The form of management letter which requires to be submitted annually to the Society by every firm authorised to conduct investment business is contained in Schedule 1 to the Solicitors (Scotland) Compliance Certificate Rules 1994. The management letter is sent to the Society along with the compliance certificate (the form of which is contained in Schedule 2 to the Compliance Certificate Rules).

The compliance certificate and management letter must be delivered to the Society within six months of the completion of each accounting period.

Management letter

There are two parts to the management letter – Part A and Part B. Part A (positive return) is completed by those firms which are authorised to conduct investment business and actually carry out investment business in the relevant period. Part B (nil return) is completed by those firms which although authorised to conduct investment business have not conducted any in the relevant period.

Before the firm's accountant can start his inspection of the firm's investment business records the firm must prepare the management letter on its own letter head which will show the scope and scale of the investment business carried out during the relevant period. The sections of the management letter are set out below.

Part A – positive return

Section 1 – extent of investment business

Under this section the firm is required to certify that it was carrying on the practice of a Scottish solicitor and that the firm's gross income did not derive wholly or mainly from investment business.

The firm is required to keep a record of its investment income which will determine whether or not the gross income of its practice is wholly or mainly derived from investment business (rule 6.5). This certification and record keeping is required as the Society cannot authorise any firm which has more than 50% of its income derived from investment business.

A firm should maintain separate accounts within the firm's ledger of both fees charged for investment business and financial services commissions received. The commission account will show the total commission received for work done under FSA and the fees account will record all fees charged in respect of investment business.

In executry and trust work it is not always possible to ascertain accurately the percentage of fee appropriate to investment work, although the Auditor of Court will split a fee for an executry between investment and general work if asked. Where a precise calculation is not possible, the undernoted percentage table can be used as a guide (*nb the following is only illustrative*).

TYPE OF BUSINESS	PROPORTION OF INCOME DERIVED FROM INVESTMENT BUSINESS
Executries	5%
Continuing trusts	10%
Corporate finance work	5%

Section 2 – Scope of investment business

In this section a firm is asked to identify from a list of nine categories of investment business what actual investment business was conducted in the relevant period.

The nine categories of investment business are as follows:

(a) **Discretionary investment management** – this is where a firm manages a portfolio (generally of stocks and shares although it could include unit trusts) in the exercise of discretion.

(b) **Non-discretionary investment management** – this is where a firm has assumed responsibility for advising or commenting on the investments comprised in a client's portfolio. It is to be noted that a firm which communicates a stockbroker's report on a portfolio to his client without commenting upon the investments therein is not an investment manager.

(c) **Advising on investments** – this means the giving of general advice on investments.

(d) **Arranging transactions in securities** – this means arranging Stock Exchange purchases and sales through stockbrokers.

(e) **Advising on and/or arranging life policies** – self-explanatory.

(f) **Advising on or arranging pensions** – self-explanatory.

(g) **Advising on or arranging other packaged products** – this means advising or arranging in relation to unit trusts and investment trust savings schemes.

(h) **Advising on or arranging corporate finance activities** – self-explanatory.

(i) **Other investment activities** – here the firm must specify any other investment activity (ie Enterprise Zone Property Trusts) which it is involved with.

Section 3 – Scale of securities transactions and investment management

This section which consists of 6 questions should only be completed by those firms which have in the relevant period carried out Stock Exchange investment transactions on behalf of clients or have acted as a discretionary portfolio manager.

In *question 1* the number of statements of terms of business provided (in relation to non-discretionary portfolio management) and written contracts (in relation to discretionary portfolio management) issued to clients in force at the date of the management letter must be shown.

In answering *question 2* the number of individual Stock Exchange transactions in excess of £100,000 effected or arranged on a non-discretionary basis in the relevant period must be shown.

In answering *question 3* the firm must show the number of portfolios managed on a discretionary basis at the date of the management letter.

In the answer to *question 4* the firm must give the total value of all the funds in all the portfolios which are managed on a discretionary basis. The value of such funds is at the date of the management letter or the value given in the last report on the portfolios sent to clients in accordance with rule 6.3.

In answering *question 5* firms must state the number of portfolios managed on a discretionary basis in excess of £100,000 at the date of the management letter.

In answering *question 6* the number of individual Stock Exchange transactions in excess of £100,000 effected or arranged on a discretionary basis in the relevant period must be shown.

Section 4 – Life policies and units in collective investment schemes

In answering question A the firm must give the number of life policies placed (both directly and indirectly through another intermediary) together with the name of the respective life office. This information will be obtainable from the detailed records which require to be kept on life policies under rule 6.6

To answer question B the firm must state the number of unit trusts placed (both directly and indirectly through another intermediary) and the names of the unit trusts companies.

Section 5 – Investment Business Training Regulations

This section must be completed as from 1 November 1995. In this section the names of those individuals within the firm who are authorised to conduct investment business in terms of the Training Regulations must be given. For each individual the following information must also be given:
(a) whether that individual has passed the Society's Investment Business Examination or been exempted from it or holds an equivalent qualification and specify that equivalent qualification; and
(b) each individual's 'starting' and 'finishing' dates (if applicable) with the firm.

Section 6 – Compliance

This declaration must be signed by a partner in the firm, usually the compliance officer.

Part B – nil return

This return is only to be completed by those firms which although authorised to conduct investment business did not carry out any such business in the relevant period. Section 2 of the nil return is the same as section 5 of the positive return and section 3 of the nil return is the same as section 6 of the positive return.

Compliance certificate

A compliance certificate prepared by the firm's accountant requires to be submitted to the Society within six months of the completion of each accounting period.

A compliance certificate must be granted by an accountant meeting the criteria contained in rule 4 of the Solicitors (Scotland) Accountants Certificate Rules 1992. The compliance certificate is often granted by the same person who grants the accountant's certificate. However before a compliance certificate can be granted the firm's accountant must have sight of the completed management letter which requires to be sent to the Society with the compliance certificate.

Before completion of the compliance certificate the firm's accountant will require to be satisfied that all record keeping systems are in place and that the procedures necessary to comply with the CBRs and Training Regulations have been followed. The main requirements which the accountant must verify are as follows:

(1)   That the firm's gross income did not derive wholly or mainly from investment business (rule 6.5).

(2)   Rule 4.4 and 4.5 – best advice and best execution – the firm must have records showing an adequate and reasonable basis for any investment recommendation. The person giving the advice must have recorded the client's personal and financial situation and investment objectives on the client fact sheet. The other records which are required to be maintained in relation to rules 4.4 and 4.5 were outlined in Part I of this workbook.

(3)   Rule 4.7 (client terms of business record) – the firm must retain a copy of all statements of terms of business provided and written contracts entered into as well as any client agreements until they all cease to be effective.

(4)   Rule 5.1 (advertisement records) – a firm under rule 5.1(7) is required to keep copies of all investment advertisements issued or approved by it for at least five years.

(5)   Rule 6.1 (transaction records) – the firm is required to maintain the transaction records required under rule 6.1(1–3) for a period of 10 years.

(6)   Rule 6.4 (client's title documents) – records require to be kept of all documents of title relating to clients' securities. Furthermore records require to be kept where a firm employs a third party to provide nominee services which must show that the third party is suitable to provide such services.

(7)   Rule 6.6 (life policies and units) – records require to be kept showing the number of life policies placed directly and indirectly with each individual office and the number of unit trusts acquired directly or indirectly with each unit trust operator.

(8)   Rule 6.7 – Records have to be maintained showing the number of transactions effected on an investment exchange other than a recognised stock exchange.

(9)   Rule 6.2 (client notification) – the information required here can be obtained by keeping copies of the relevant contract notes.

(10) Rule 6.3 (managed portfolios report) – records require to be kept showing that where a firm has acted as portfolio manager it has sent to clients reports on their portfolios at least once a year.

(11) Investment Business Training Regulations – records have to be maintained which show that the firm complied with the Investment Business Training Regulations.

In order for a compliance certificate and management letter to be completed it is essential for a firm to have access to accurate, up-to-date information to be able to show that at all times the firm complied with the Society's Rules on the Conduct of Investment Business.

PART VI – DISCIPLINE

As the Society authorises firms to conduct investment business any breach of requirements of any of the Investment Business Rules is the responsibility of the relevant partners in the firm against whom any disciplinary action will be taken by the Society. Rule 7.3 of the CBRs provides that any breach of the Investment Business Rules may be treated as professional misconduct. If any of the Rules are breached the matter is considered by the Society's Investment Business Committee. This Committee is independent of the Society's Council and has 25% lay representation. The Investment Business Committee considers complaints of breach of the Rules from clients of firms and also breaches of the Rules which have been notified by the Society's own inspecting accountants and a firm's accountant.

Complaints from the public

The stages in the investigation of an investment business complaint from a member of the public are as follows:
(1) A firm against whom a complaint is made must firstly investigate the complaint promptly and thoroughly and, where practicable, this investigation should be carried out by a partner not concerned in the action or inaction complained of;
(2) the firm must then inform the complainer that it is open to him to report the matter to the Investment Business Committee;
(3) if the Investment Business Committee receives the complaint the following options are open to the Committee as to how it disposes of the complaint:
   (a) if the complaint is not made out it will be dismissed with no further action;
   (b) if the complaint is deemed by the Committee to be made out but not to amount to professional misconduct a letter may be sent to the solicitor responsible for the breach in question (or for the supervision of the member of staff concerned), deploring or regretting the conduct in question;
   (c) if the complaint is deemed to amount to an inadequate professional service being provided to the client the Committee can:
      (i) order the firm to reduce or waive its fee;
      (ii) order the firm to sort out the client's affairs at the firm's expense; or
      (iii) order the firm to take any other action which the Committee may specify;
   (d) if the complaint is deemed to amount to professional misconduct then the solicitor may be reprimanded and a note of this will be made on the solicitor's record;

(e) if the complaint is very serious the matter may be referred to the Scottish Solicitor's Discipline Tribunal. If the Tribunal finds there has been professional misconduct it can fine the solicitor to a maximum of £10,000; it can restrict or suspend the firm's Investment Business Certificate; it can order that the solicitor is suspended from practice or it can strike the solicitor off the roll.

If the complainer is not happy with the Committee's disposal of a complaint the complainer can refer the matter to the Scottish Legal Services Ombudsman who oversees the Society's handling of complaints.

Where rule breaches are identified by the Society's inspecting accountant or indeed the firm's own accountant the Investment Business Committee may impose any of the sanctions mentioned above and in addition may require remedial action and changes/improvements to the firm's office systems and a re-inspection may be ordered.

Other powers

In various circumstances the Society can suspend or withdraw a firm's Investment Business Certificate. Such circumstances are:

(1) where the firm ceases to practise as solicitors;
(2) where the firm ceases to comply with the Investment Business Training Regulations;
(3) where the firm becomes insolvent;
(4) where the firm does not pay the fee for authorisation within 30 days of it being charged;
(5) where the firm does not deliver a management letter and compliance certificate within six months of the completion of the accounting period;
(6) where the Council is satisfied that after a reasonable enquiry investors would not be adequately protected if the firm's Investment Business Certificate was not withdrawn/suspended; and
(7) where the firm's gross income is derived wholly or mainly from investment business.

A firm cannot conduct investment business while its investment business certificate is suspended and not only would it be professional misconduct to do so but any such business conducted in these circumstances would also amount to a criminal offence.

Appendix 5

Client dissatisfaction*

At the present time it is accepted that anyone involved in providing a service is likely to find themselves liable to be faced with a dissatisfied client. The purpose of this paper is to look at the setting up of a procedure within an office to deal with this and the ways in which this should be handled should a client's concern or dissatisfaction turn into a formal complaint. This procedure should apply whether the dissatisfaction is made known directly to the firm or whether the complaint comes via the Law Society's complaints procedure, but ideally the aim should be to deal with the matter within the practice at an early stage to the client's satisfaction or understanding thus increasing the prospect of retaining the client. Research findings show that if dissatisfaction is resolved, 70% of customers will do further business. If it is not resolved quickly, 90% will not do further business. The following procedure is capable of being adapted to deal with the client's concerns before they become complaints. The desirability of doing so is underpinned by the statistic that only 4% of unhappy customers make their concerns known, 96% simply go elsewhere.

Handling a dissatisfied client

It is considered that the most effective way of dealing with this problem is to make one person within a firm responsible for dealing with concerned clients. The person is known as the client relations partner. This is the person to whom any indication of dissatisfaction should immediately be passed. Clearly this is a problem for a sole practitioner. A possible solution is for a sole practitioner to agree to 'swap' such problems with another sole practitioner although it is understood this may not be acceptable. Another possibility may be to seek assistance through the local faculty.

The role of the client relations partner is to try to resolve the problem in an appropriate way. It is suggested that a second or reserve client relations partner should be appointed in case the problem relates to the client relations partner.

How to deal with the matter

1. On receipt of the expression of dissatisfaction the client relations partner should immediately acknowledge receipt of the correspondence

*Reproduced from *Better Client Care and Practice*
© The Law Society of Scotland

197

to the client and indicate that he or she will be dealing with it. It will normally be appropriate to indicate to the client that the papers are being considered and a further response will be sent within seven to ten days.

2. Having acknowledged the problem the client relations partner should in the first instance obtain the file and consider it. He or she should also speak to the solicitor or solicitors who have been involved in dealing with the matter giving rise to the complaint.

3. Having done this the client relations partner should be able to form a view of the basis of the concerns expressed and whether they are justified or not.

4. Whether or not the concern is justified, it is suggested that the client should either be invited to a meeting to discuss the matter or given the opportunity of airing their grievance by telephone. It is often the case that what the client may have put forward in writing as the concerns, are not in fact what the actual concerns are, and indeed dissatisfaction may come about as a result of either bad communication or misunderstanding.

5. If a meeting or a discussion is to take place about the matter then the client relations partner should approach the matter positively—if the concerns are in some way justified, consideration should be given to appeasing the client either by way of apology or some form of redress (eg reduction in fees).

6. If the concerns are not justified try to explain to the client what the difficulties are and why the concerns are not justified.

7. Whether or not the concerns are justified, it is appropriate to follow the meeting or discussion with a letter to the client either confirming matters have been resolved or setting out the reason why no action is appropriate, or, if action is appropriate, what steps will be taken.

Advising staff

If a client relations partner is appointed then all members of staff within the firm should be advised as to the identity of the client relations partner. All members of staff should be further advised that if a client indicates at any stage dissatisfaction with the way their affairs are being dealt with then the identity of the client relations partner should be disclosed.

All staff, particularly qualified solicitors, should be advised that if they receive a letter of dissatisfaction either directly from the client or from the Law Society, then the matter should immediately be drawn to the attention of the client relations partner.

Advice for the client relations partner

There are two golden rules in dealing with dissatisfied clients which client relations partners should always bear in mind. The first of these is simply—do not delay in dealing with the matter. In many instances concerns can become more serious than they actually are because the problems are not addressed quickly.

Secondly, a client relations partner should not assume on receipt of a letter of dissatisfaction that there is no substance to it. A client relations partner should, in each case, consider the papers and investigate the matter.

It is worth noting that it has been suggested in some quarters that it is appropriate for solicitors to draw attention to the existence of a procedure for dealing with dissatisfaction in any literature advertising the firm to clients and it has also been suggested that clients should be made aware at the commencement of business that there is such a procedure within the firm. This is a matter for individual firms to take a decision upon but if the use of the word 'complaints' is a problem because it suggests to clients that there might be a cause for complaint, it need not necessarily be used. It is quite possible simply to tell clients that the firm wants to know when a client has a question or concern about a particular transaction and that it has a mechanism for addressing such questions or concerns.

Points to remember

- Always attempt to resolve client dissatisfaction within the practice.

- Ensure all staff are aware of the identity of the client relations partner.

- Ensure dissatisfied clients are passed to the client relations partner at the earliest possible moment.

- Acknowledge receipt immediately. Advise of action being taken.

- Invite the dissatisfied client to discuss the matter either in person or by telephone.

- Ensure that information received from and given to the client is confirmed in writing.

- If justification is found for the concerns consider appeasing the dissatisfied client.

- If the concerns are not justified explain to the client both verbally and in writing why this is so.

- Ensure matters are resolved at the earliest possible moment.

- Communicate to clients the firm's willingness to answer questions or deal with concerns the client may have at any time during the course of a matter.

Index